Prescription Positive Rx

A Great Way to Live... and Live Longer

***The SECRET** to unleashing the power of your conscious **and** subconscious mind to create health and longevity.*

Special Foreword By:
Deborah F. Harding, M.D.
Founder/CEO, Harding Anti-Aging Center

RICHARD C. HUSEMAN, PH.D.

Equity Press

Cover design by Zulema C. Seguel

Huseman, Richard C.
Prescription positive: a great way to live... and live longer

Richard C. Huseman, Ph.D.
p. cm.
ISBN: 978-0-9896275-1-1

1. Health & Wellness 2. Healthcare 3. Longevity & Health
4. Positivity & Positive Mindset 5. Placebo Effect 6. Human Perception
7. Thinking and Thought

Printed in the United States of America

Praise for Prescription Positive

"In a time when our healthcare system is failing, Dick Huseman offers a solution that is proof positive to increase the quantity of years and quality of life. With crystal clarity ***Prescription Positive*** *not only reveals the power of the mind, but what the mind can do to improve overall wellbeing. Rightly applying the six positive prescriptions will alter the course of illness, reduce risk for disease and bend the trajectory of American healthcare. As a physician and healthcare executive, this book is a "must read" for anyone who seeking a better life now, and in the future."*

Monica Reed, MD
CEO, Celebration Health
Author, **The Creation Health Breakthrough**

"As a physician and surgeon, I have learned that the power of positive thinking is more important than most people believe. There are times in my practice where if I realized that a patient was going into surgery thinking negatively, I would cancel the procedure and try to counsel them to consider other therapies. The power of positive belief and the RX+ Scripts provided in Dr. Huseman's book are not only something I intend to recommend to my patients... they are something that I intend to use to make me a better person and physician."

David A. Heimansohn, M.D.
Cardiovascular Surgeon
St. Vincent Medical Group

"While the idea of one's subconscious affecting the outcome of illness has been put forward by others, your book clearly traces the path of reason that allows one to grasp this complex phenomenon. Congratulations on creating a pathway to health that should be embraced by not only the public but healthcare providers, as well. If only doctors would begin to view an introspective exam of their patients instead of just the external analysis, a new generation of pharmaceutical formulary could evolve from a Prescription of Positive Beliefs about oneself!."

Richard A. Conn, M.D.
Orthopedic Surgeon
Southern Bone & Joint Specialists
Hattiesburg, Mississippi

"Having been a family physician for the better part of my life, treating people in various degrees of "health," and disease, I have seen the power of positive thinking and beliefs firsthand. I have seen patients who were given only weeks to live somehow (miraculously?) live for years due to their very positive attitude. Conversely, I have had patients who, with a difficult diagnosis and with therapy that would work well for the great majority, fall into a "gloom and doom" attitude that led to a shortened life. Our attitudes and beliefs surely help determine our longevity and in great part, control how one's body reacts to the stresses of health and everyday life. Dr. Huseman's book, ***Prescription Positive****, is a must read, not only for the general public, but especially for all who care for the infirm. It should be read by every medical student and healthcare provider."*

Mark H. Belfer, M.D.
Chief Medical Officer
Greater Rochester Independent Practice Association

"Dick Huseman's ***Prescription Positive*** *is a thought-provoking, insightful book. It not only encourages people to take ownership of their own health, it gives them the tools to tap their conscious and subconscious minds to promote true wellness and longevity. As a strategic leader in one of the top 15 health systems in the country, I believe that a positive mindset is crucial to staying healthy and making the most out of life. Prescription Positive provides the blueprint."*

Scott Wooten
Senior Vice President and Chief Financial Officer
Alegent Creighton Health

"Dr. Huseman has given us an insightful, thought-provoking book that illustrates the POWER of POSITIVE BELIEFS. As a lifelong Marine, I have seen firsthand the incredible results an individual can achieve with a positive mental outlook and a can-do attitude. History is replete with examples from the battlefield to the ball field where the underdogs prevailed because of their positive mindsets, because when there is a positive mindset, anything is possible. Dr. Huseman provides the proof that POSITIVE BELIEFS can be harnessed to give us healthier and longer lives."

Colonel Samuel T. Studdard
United States Marine Corps (retired)

"One of the reasons I became a concierge physician was so that I could develop stronger relationships with my patients. I wanted to look beyond test results and examinations to get to know the people who sought my help for their healthcare. I wanted to learn more about their lives and lifestyles, because life is so much more than the number of days we are on this Earth. It is about how we choose to approach life, and all of its challenges and opportunities. Prescription Positive provides a framework for how you can leverage the power of your conscious and subconscious mind for a healthy and fulfilling life. The book is packed with real-world strategies for enhancing the power of your mind that you can start using immediately."

Ivan Castro, M.D.
Concierge Physician
Winter Park, Florida

"Anyone who practices clinical medicine cannot deny a mind-body connection with health and wellness. There is so much to be explored in this area, and Dr. Huseman has certainly pointed out the myriad possibilities in his book ***Prescription Positive****. In my practice, I have seen old, sick 40 year olds, and young, healthy 80 year olds – the power of the mind, attitude, and force of personality and personal will are truly amazing and humbling. I would especially recommend the reader pay close attention to the chapter on dealing with stress and anxiety, and also the section regarding the power of a positive attitude and outlook. I would heartily encourage this book be read by all who claim to want to take care of patients—from new students and interns, to wizened attendings and those involved with administration, insurance, and even government regulations. Those who would scoff should do so at their own risk – there is much to be learned in this area, and much to be gained in taking better care of people by helping them take charge and take better care of themselves!"*

Stephen Jarrard, MD, FACS
Chief of Surgery and Chief Medical Officer
Mountain Lakes Medical Center
Clayton, Georgia

"Like me, once you read this book, you will not look at healthcare, and its related costs, the same way again. For the cost of a thought, this book unlocks the mind and allows it to form a belief system that affords the potential for a healthier life. Dr. Huseman's ***Prescription Positive*** *gives you the opportunity for an extraordinary happy and long life, and that is priceless!"*

Gail H. Johnson
Walt Disney World Program Executive (retired)

Dedicated to the associates, friends and family who have provided their insight, expertise, support and guidance to me over the years.

Most specifically, this book is dedicated to:

My wife, Carolyn,

Our sons, Doug and Rich,

Their wives, Joyce and Erika,

Our seven grandchildren,

Tyler, Callie, Brett, Chase

Justin, Brennon and Connor,

And to all of the generations they represent.

"We cannot change the inevitable.
The only thing we can do is play on the
one string we have, and that is our ***attitude****.*

I am convinced that life is 10%
what happens to me
and 90% how I react to it."

Pastor Charles R. Swindoll
Founder of *Insight for Living*

ACKNOWLEDGEMENTS

This book is quite a departure for me. I never expected that my professional coaching work within the healthcare industry would yield such intriguing fruit. Many people have contributed to this work, more often than not by forcing me to question my own beliefs about health, wellness and longevity. Specifically, I would like to thank Dr. Ivan Castro, my concierge physician and Dr. Eric Janowitz, my chiropractor, for their help and guidance with my own personal health goals. Similarly, I would like to thank Michelle Dillman, my personal fitness coach for the last ten years and my pharmacists Chris Laursen and Catherine Le. More recently, I am grateful to Dr. Deborah Harding, founder and CEO of the Harding Anti-Aging Institute, for her input into my anti-aging regimen.

I also wish to specifically thank Martin Stickley, Ph.D. for reading and providing comments on almost every draft of the book. Thanks also to Kevin Rose for providing some practical examples for how the power of the brain can be prompted, especially when it comes to reducing pain. Many others also took time out of hectic schedules to review the manuscript and provide their suggestions and comments including David Heimansohn, M.D., Deborah Harding, M.D., Stephen Swinney, M.D., Mark Belfer, M.D., Monica Reed, M.D., Richard Conn, M.D, Stephen Jarrard, M.D., Scott Wooten, Colonel Samuel "Ted" Studdard, Dick Gilson, Ph.D., Gail Johnson, Jerry Pierce, Anne Curtis, Bill Cooper, Dave & Charlotte Nielson, Harry & Carol Smith, Lex and Carol Wood, Shirley Pipkin and Cecily Crossman.

On the literary side, as always, my thanks to Zulema Seguel for her assistance in conceptualizing, writing, editing and formatting this book… one of many we have worked on together. Finally, and most importantly, I would like to thank my family for their continuing love and support in all my endeavors.

Table of Contents

Part **THREE**:
The Power of a Positive Approach to Life [37]

Part **FOUR**:
Your Prescription Positive [65]

Foreword
By Deborah F. Harding, M.D.

As a physician, I have seen firsthand how many people choose to live their lives. I have seen them strive for peak health, persevere through illness, and, when the time came, gracefully meet their end. I have seen the extraordinary power of the body's innate ability to heal, and the even more extraordinary power of the spirit's will to live. I am also intimately familiar with the fragility of life, and how in the blink of an eye, the health and vitality we so easily take for granted can be taken away.

My responsibilities as a physician are many and varied, but my true vocation stems from a single root desire. I want to help people. I have dedicated my time, energy and effort – undertaken years of advanced education, experience and training – all in order to help people face some of life's most difficult challenges.

At the beginning of my career, much of my focus was on people whose health was already in jeopardy. After earning my medical degree from Southern Illinois University School of Medicine, I specialized in Internal Medicine, spending many hours working in the Intensive Care Units (ICU) at Orlando Health Hospitals, attending patients who required the most critical care. In my private practice, I oversaw the medical needs of a number of nursing homes, working with those who could no longer care for themselves, and who were in their final stages of life.

What struck me in those early years was how often my patients sought treatment for issues that were preventable. The Centers for Disease Control and Prevention estimate that nearly 80% of all illnesses are preventable. Today, preventable illness accounts for eight of the nine leading categories of death. My own practice of medicine mirrored these data points, and it peaked my interest in "preventative health" long before the term became common healthcare jargon.

Several years ago, I branched out from my Internal Medicine field of study and started working in the new area of sleep disorder medicine. During this time, my passion for the practice of preventative medicine was recognized by the Florida Hospital healthcare system, and I was offered a role in building their flagship hospital's executive wellness program at Celebration Hospital. This work inspired me to continue my education and, in 2006, I became certified by Cenegenics Medical Institute in Age Management Medicine. Founded in 1997, Cenegenics pioneered the development of Age Management Medicine (AMM), and is recognized as the leading authority in this rapidly growing and emerging field. A year later, I also became certified by the American Academy of Anti-Aging and Regenerative Medicine, the world leader in anti-aging education and training.

Today, I am the founder and president of the Harding Anti-Aging Center based in Central Florida. I created the center because I believe in maximizing the health and wellness of my patients. My goal is to act as the catalyst that motivates and empowers people to embrace a healthier lifestyle, experience optimal health, and live the longest life possible.

It is in the pursuit of this goal that I met the author of this book, Richard Huseman, Ph.D. Dick came to our center to take part in our Anti-Aging Concierge Health Program. In my initial one-on-one appointment with him, he told me about his interest in anti-aging, particularly when it came to maintaining a positive attitude as part of his regimen of staying healthy and living longer. At a subsequent session, he gave me the opportunity to review a draft of his manuscript, and I found the concepts he set forth resonating with many of my own beliefs about positivity and longevity.

For example, I have read other literature about the power of the placebo in healing, and the complexity behind how taking a "sugar pill" translates into real physiological change is mind-boggling. While most physicians will acknowledge it as a real phenomenon, few can explain it. However, Dick builds a clear and concise argument that while we may not understand how placebos work, they do work, and that is what matters. His stories and examples of the placebo effect are the bedrock for why Dick believes a positive mindset is such a critical component to securing health and longevity. **PRESCRIPTION POSITIVE: A GREAT WAY TO LIVE... AND LIVE LONGER** makes a compelling case that **belief** is a potent force in helping us live longer and healthier lives – something I believe needs to be embraced not only by the public at large, but by the healthcare industry itself.

In my own experience as a physician, I know people want to live longer and happier lives. That is why they come through my door. They want me to help them get the most out of life for as long as they can. This inherent positive outlook on life motivates people to take care of themselves, and take action to protect their health and vitality. The RX+ Scripts that Dick sets forth in Part Four of the book are powerful tools to help people leverage a positive mindset in their own lives. Whether it is through "**SELF-ACCOUNTABILITY,**" "**AN ATTITUDE OF GRATITUDE,**" or a "**FOCUS ON POSITIVE RELATIONSHIPS,**" people can take their RX+ "health supplement" any time –

24 hours a day, 7 days a week and 365 days a year – to tap into their own positivity health potential.

I have always been a positive person. I believe that having a positive attitude is a key ingredient to living a full and happy life. As a physician, I can provide you with data on your key health metrics. I can help you develop a medically sound plan to support your health and longevity. I can make sure you are being proactive in all the right ways to keep your body running at peak efficiency. But, this book, **PRESCRIPTION POSITIVE: A GREAT WAY TO LIVE... AND LIVE LONGER**, can be a great addition to your longevity regimen. It can enable you to tap into the power of your conscious and subconscious mind through the **POWER OF POSITIVE BELIEF** to maintain your health, and enjoy a long, happy life.

My prescription is to read this book. In my professional opinion, a dose of **PRESCRIPTION POSITIVE** is just what the doctor ordered.

Deborah F. Harding, M.D.
Founder & President
Harding Anti-Aging Center
Orlando, Florida

INTRODUCTION

It's all in the genes. The vast majority of people today believe their lives are controlled by their genetic code. Most of us attribute our abilities (or disabilities), our health (or illness), potential (or lack of potential) to the genes we inherited from our parents. Our educational system reinforces this – from elementary school through graduate school (even medical school). We have been conditioned to believe that our lives, and especially our health are controlled by the genes we inherit, and that we are subservient to the power of our DNA, especially when it comes to our health. You hear it all the time:

- "The men in my family have all died from heart attacks before the age of 50."
- "Cancer runs in my family."
- "My father and my sister are both diabetics."

These statements and their repetition illustrate the power we attribute to our genetic code, permitting us to feel like victims, powerless against our genetic fate. **THIS BELIEF HAS ONE POWERFUL CONSEQUENCE. IT ALLOWS US TO SHIRK INDIVIDUAL RESPONSIBILITY FOR OUR HEALTH AND WELL-BEING.** This fatalistic mindset that we are simply doomed to follow our genetic programming is not only unfortunate – it is self-fulfilling and completely wrong.

Advances in physics and cellular biology are calling into question the very foundations of conventional medicine. A new understanding of cell science suggests it is **ENVIRONMENT – MORE SPECIFICALLY OUR "PERCEPTION" OF OUR ENVIRONMENT** – that influences the activity of our genes. Our perception of our environment controls our behavior. Since perceptions are relative and subjective, it is more accurate to refer to our "perceptions" as "beliefs." That is the bottom line of what this book is all about. **IT IS NOT SO MUCH YOUR GENES, BUT YOUR BELIEFS THAT CONTROL YOUR HEALTH AND WELL-BEING!**

Your beliefs have far reaching consequences, both positive and negative. Beliefs affect your self-worth, the relationships you develop, the way you perform at work, and especially your mental and physical health. Your mind and the beliefs it creates determine far more than most of us currently understand. This book, **Prescription Positive: A Great Way to Live... and Live Longer**, is about the power of positive beliefs and how our beliefs impact our health.

The Will to Live

"Aging is mainly psychological, not biological. Everything in our society tells us that as we grow older, we will lose our mental powers, our health, our sexual capacities. We start believing it all, and because we believe it, it begins to come true. But it doesn't have to be this way. Seventy-five percent of so called aging results from a self-fulfilling prophecy."

Dr. Arnold A. Hutschnecker
Author of ***The Will to LIve***

THE INTENTION

This book is intended to promote wellness and longevity in those people who are willing to accept both the **OPPORTUNITY** and **RESPONSIBILITY** inherent in taking active control over their health. The concepts presented here are only as effective and valuable as the reader's ability to leverage them to their own benefit.

If you believe you are currently unwell, this book can offer you insights into coping with your disease, injury or illness. But, in truth, this book is primarily for people who consider themselves well, even if they have occasional or even persistent doubts about their health. What this book seeks to do is bolster our inherent sense of invincibility. Most of us have an indomitable belief that we deserve to be healthy and well. We recognize that illness is an unnatural state, and that health is intended to be our natural condition.

That is not to say that we have not encountered illness, be it heartburn or heartache, backache and neck pain, unusual bowel function, strange sensations, numbness in parts of our bodies, realizations of our physical limits, and a plethora of other predicaments. We have experienced them before, and we will experience them again. They can be unpleasant, disturbing, personal and even noxious experiences that can test the limits of our beliefs about our state of health.

PRESCRIPTION POSITIVE is written to be a support when our sense of wellness is challenged. When we come up against the surging mass of both real and perceived threats to our wellness and longevity – threats often reinforced by our healthcare system – our innate perceptions of wellness can be overwhelmed. This book attempts to level the playing field, and help us rekindle hope and purpose when it comes to securing our own health and longevity.

This book is no way intended to preclude the need for medical intervention by an appropriate healthcare provider. If you need medical care, you should seek it aggressively. However, the concepts in this book can serve as an important adjunct to your healthcare process, motivating you to be an active participant in choosing the right healthcare providers to assist you, and take responsibility for rationally considering your treatment options. **WE ALL NEED TO BE FAR MORE SOPHISTICATED HEALTHCARE CONSUMERS.** This book is intended to enlighten and challenge you to take charge of your own health and longevity, as it is both your right and obligation to do.

THE FORMAT

The book begins with a discussion of the current state of healthcare in this country. We look at what it is we really want from healthcare and how, despite the fact the U.S. spends twice as much on healthcare than other developed countries, we are not living longer or healthier lives.

We then move to an examination of the power of belief. Using the examples of the placebo effect, we provide evidence that more than anything else, **IT IS THE MIND THAT DETERMINES THE STATE OF OUR HEALTH**. Scientific data and research proves time and time again that **THE HISTORY OF MEDICINE IS ACTUALLY THE HISTORY OF THE PLACEBO EFFECT**, and by harnessing the biology of belief, we have the key to unlocking true wellness and longevity.

Next, we look at how a positive mindset can help us live longer and happier lives. By understanding how the brain influences our perceptions of the world (both positively and negatively), we can consciously choose to focus on the positive, creating the level of health and wellness we seek in our lives.

Finally, we offer six prescriptions ("Scripts") that you can use to start leveraging positivity in your life right away, allowing you to harness your beliefs to secure true health and longevity today.

To help you navigate, the parts of the book are sectioned as follows:

Part ONE: **THE CURRENT STATE OF HEALTHCARE**
Part TWO: **THE POWER OF POSITIVE BELIEF**

Part THREE: **The Power of a Positive Approach to Life**
Part FOUR: **Your Prescription Positive**

The ultimate purpose of this book is to allow you to activate and leverage the power you have over your own health and wellness. You have both the opportunity and responsibility to determine your own destiny, regardless of your genetic programming. The answer is not some elite exercise program or nutritional panacea, but the simple act of **HARNESSING THE POWER OF YOUR MIND** to keep you well and to restore your health when necessary. By the time you finish reading this book, you will have all the tools you need to ensure a long, active and healthy life. **After all, as we will demonstrate, it is all in your mind!**

Part **ONE**

THE CURRENT STATE OF HEALTHCARE

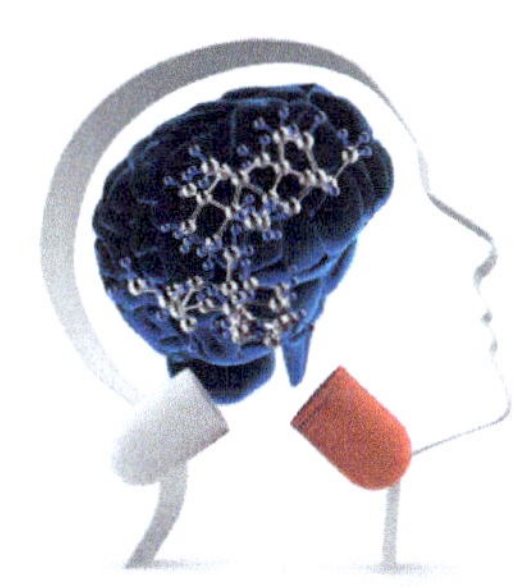

Chapter ONE

What Do You Really Want From Healthcare?

A few years ago, I was at a healthcare conference in Los Angeles. There were about 1,000 physicians, nurses and other healthcare practitioners in the room. The speaker that morning began by saying, "I'm going to start things a little differently today. Before I begin my presentation, I want you to talk to the person next to you, and come up with what you think people **REALLY** want from our healthcare system."

The room buzzed as people talked amongst themselves, and after a few minutes, the speaker halted the discussion to have people share some of their answers:

- "I want healthcare that is safe and effective."
- "I want healthcare that is close by."
- "I want healthcare that is affordable."

After listening to several comments, the speaker instructed the audience again. "This time I want you to think what it is you **REALLY**, **REALLY** want from healthcare." Again, there was a buzz in the room, but not quite as loud as before. When the speaker readdressed the group, he invited a few more people to share their responses.

- "I want my doctor to be able to spend time with me, and not just be another face in the crowd of too many patients."
- "I want to have some control of how I spend my healthcare dollars, including who I see and even explore alternative methods of treatment."
- "I don't want my insurance company determining what kind of treatment I receive."

Then, the speaker asked the question one more time. "What is it that you **REALLY, REALLY, REALLY** want from healthcare?" This time, there was only a low hum in the room as everyone muttered among themselves about what answer the speaker was obviously fishing for.

Finally, one man raised his hand. "**WHAT I REALLY WANT FROM HEALTHCARE IS NOT TO NEED IT.**" That was the right answer, and it is the truth for most people.

WHAT THE MAJORITY OF US WANT FROM HEALTHCARE IS NOT TO NEED IT!

You may smile at this answer, but when you consider the big picture of healthcare in the United States today, and how ineffective our healthcare system can be, you will quickly understand why most of us should really, really want to not need it.

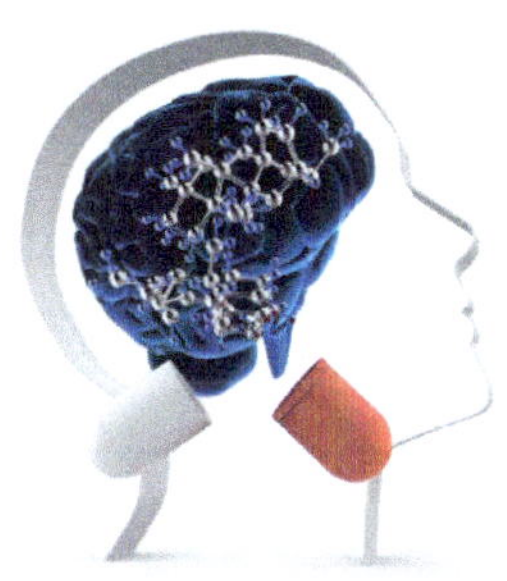

CHAPTER TWO

THE UNBALANCED COST/BENEFIT RATIO

Some might assume that we experience shortcomings in healthcare in this country because we are not spending enough money on medical treatment. The exact opposite is true. The United States spends more on healthcare than any other country in the world.

THE REAL PROBLEM IS, for all the money we spend on healthcare, we are not receiving any better care than people in the rest of the developing world. **IN FACT, THE CARE WE RECEIVE IS FAR WORSE.**

AS YOU SEE FROM THE TABLE ON THE FOLLOWING PAGE, THE U.S. SPENDS ALMOST DOUBLE THE AMOUNT ON HEALTHCARE AS CANADA, FRANCE AND GERMANY; far more when compared to the rest of the countries on the list. Given PPACA (i.e., Obamacare) and other expected changes to healthcare policies in this country, the amount we spend on healthcare as a percent of Gross Domestic Product (GDP) is only going to increase in future years, far outpacing the rest of the world.

Health Expenditures/Life Expectancy
Comparison of U.S. to Select Other Countries, 2009/2010

Country	Expenditure per Capita	Expenditure (% of GDP)	Life Expectancy at 60	Life Expectancy at birth
Australia	$3,441	8.7%	25	82
Canada	$4,404	11.3%	24	81
China	$379	5.1%	19	74
France	$4,021	11.9%	25	81
Germany	$4,332	11.6%	23	80
Japan	$3,204	9.5%	26	83
Russia	$998	5.1%	17	68
Sweden	$3,757	9.6%	24	81
United Kingdom	$3,480	9.6%	23	80
United States	**$8,362**	**17.9%**	**23**	**79**

Data from World Health Organization's Global Health Observatory

To help put the cost of healthcare in this country into perspective, consider the cost of cleaning up after Hurricane Sandy. Many were shocked at that $60 billion price tag. More shocking is that we spent almost that amount on healthcare **LAST WEEK**! We spend more every year on artificial knees and hips than Hollywood collects at the box office. That is a lot of movie tickets.

All of this exorbitant cost might be worth it except for one critical fact… **AMERICAN CITIZENS DON'T LIVE ANY LONGER THAN PEOPLE FROM OTHER COUNTRIES.** Our life expectancy at birth is actually the **LOWEST** among major countries after Russia and China. The questions we should be asking ourselves are:

- What are we really paying for?
- Why should we continue to pay so much for healthcare if it isn't doing us much good?
- If traditional healthcare isn't providing major benefits to our health, is there something else that can?

A Cultural Issue

America has often been accused of being a culture infused with hedonism (i.e., the pursuit of pleasure). We continue to try and improve our lives by obtaining more and more and more. This trend can even be seen in our relationship with healthcare. More healthcare is always better, and this will remain so as long as:

- Payment incentives are aligned towards more care,
- Legal oversight and concerns about defensive medicine are aligned toward giving more care,
- Patients seem to want more care, and
- There is no really reliable evidence about what care is the right care;

This trend will keep pushing our country in the direction of prescribing and providing more and more medical care. If you think the United States is paying too much for healthcare today, consider the table below.

ESTIMATED U.S. ANNUAL HEALTH COST PER PERSON

Year	Cost
2010	$8,362
2020	$13,709
2030	$25,563
2040	$46,832
2050	$81,499

Data from documentary "Money and Medicine," directed by Roger Weisberg (2012)

There is no way our country can continue to pay the high price of healthcare as time goes on. Physician compensation, tort reform, insurance premiums – every facet of healthcare needs to be examined.

50% of our healthcare cost is WASTE.

"The Price of Excess:
Identifying Waste In Healthcare Spending"
PricewaterhouseCoopers' Health Research Institute (2010)

THERE MUST BE A BETTER WAY

We in the U.S. are spending nearly **TWICE AS MUCH PER CAPITA, YET OUR LIFE EXPECTANCY IS LOWER THAN OTHER DEVELOPED COUNTRIES.** This is not effective healthcare. The medical community and we as healthcare consumers are not focusing on the right things to promote complete health and wellness.

The next section of the book provides a concentrated focus on an aspect of healthcare that is often left sidelined and ignored. This critical aspect of wellness is sometimes "talked at," but rarely leveraged to its fullest potential in terms of promoting wellness and/or treating disease/illness. Medical professionals have known about it for many centuries. Theologians, philosophers and spiritualists have known about it far longer than that. The most ancient of healing practices is still one of the most important: **THE POWER OF POSITIVE BELIEF.**

Part **TWO**

The Power of Positive Belief

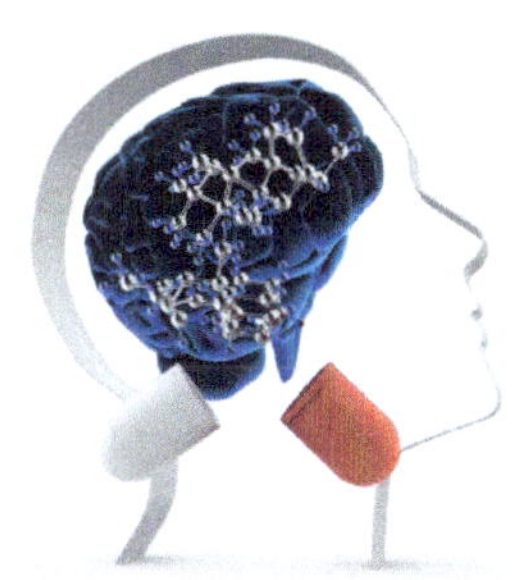

Chapter THREE

The Power of Belief and the Placebo Effect

In the early days of scientific psychology, we had a very simple picture of how the brain and the body communicated. First, certain parts of the body – the sensory organs, such as the eyes and ears – provided information to the brain via the sensory nerves. Then, after the brain sorted out what to do on the basis of this information, the brain sent the command on to the muscles by means of motor neurons. Understanding of physiology and anatomy increased, and it became clear that the situation was far more complex.

To start with, the "five senses" of vision, hearing, taste, touch and smell turned out to be much more elaborate than was previously thought. Touch, for example, is not a single process, but a combination of many different ones; various kinds of receptors in the skin are designed to detect different types of stimuli, such as heat, pressure and chemicals. **Also, it has become clear that the brain does not just receive information from the outside world but also gathers information from a rich array of sensory nerves that permeate our internal organs.** The information they convey to the brain is vital in coordinating many physiological processes, even though this information rarely becomes the object of our conscious attention.

Scientists have also made the discovery that some information about the internal state of the body is conveyed to the brain not via sensory nerves, but via **CHEMICALS** in the blood stream. Many of these molecular messengers are secreted by white blood cells whose main role is to help the body fight infection. **THIS HAS LED SOME BIOLOGISTS TO ARGUE THAT THE IMMUNE SYSTEM IS ITSELF A KIND OF SENSORY ORGAN.** Just as the eyes detect visual information about the outside world, so the various components of the immune system are continually monitoring the inside of our bodies for signs of infection, and telling the brain where they find them.

The discovery that we possess internal senses as well as external ones is paralleled by the finding that the motor neurons are not the only means by which the brain sends its messages back to the rest of the body. **BESIDES TELLING THE MUSCLES HOW TO MOVE, THE BRAIN CAN ALSO INSTRUCT IMMUNE CELLS TO CHANGE THEIR ACTIVITY.** Certain parts of the brain are designed to secrete certain chemicals back into the blood stream, and some of these chemical messengers are picked up by the white blood cells, which can alter their behavior accordingly. As we learn more about the ways in which the brain communicates with the rest of the body, it is becoming clear that mental processes need not start with external perception and end in external movement. Some can originate and terminate in events deep inside our body.

How the Mind Controls the Body

The following quote is taken from a book written by Dr. Bruce H. Lipton entitled, **The Biology of Belief: Unleashing the Power of Consciousness, Matter & Miracles** (2008).

> *My insights into how beliefs control biology are grounded in my studies of cloned endothelial cells, the cells that line the blood vessels. The endothelial cells I grew in culture monitor their world closely and change their behavior based on information they pick up from the environment. When I provided nutrients, the cells would gravitate toward those nutrients with the cellular equivalent of open arms.*

The primary switch I was studying has a protein receptor that responds to histamine, a molecule that the body uses in a way that is equivalent to a local emergency alarm. I found that there are two varieties of switches, H1 and H2, that respond to the same histamine signal. When activated, switches with H1 histamine receptors evoke a ***protection response****, the type of behavior revealed by cells in toxin-containing culture dishes. Switches containing H2 histamine receptors evoke a* ***growth response*** *to histamine, similar to the behavior of cells cultured in the presence of nutrients.*

I subsequently learned that the body's system-wide emergency response signal, adrenaline, also had switches sporting two different adrenaline-sensing receptors, called ***alpha*** *and* ***beta****. The adrenaline receptors provoked the exact same cell behaviors as those elicited by histamine. When the adrenal* ***alpha-receptor*** *is part of an IMP switch, it provokes a protection response when adrenaline is perceived. When the* ***beta-receptor*** *is part of the switch, the same adrenaline signal activates a growth response.*

All that was interesting, ***but the most exciting finding was when I simultaneously introduced both histamine and adrenaline into my tissue cultures****. I found that adrenaline signals, released by the central nervous system, override the influence of histamine signals that are produced locally. This is where the politics of the community described earlier come in to play. Which order would you follow? If you want to keep your job you'll snap to the CEO's orders. There is a similar priority built into our biology, which requires cells to follow instructions from the head honcho nervous system, even if those signals are in conflict with local stimuli.*

I was excited by my experiments because I believed that they revealed on the single-cell level a truth for multicellular organisms – ***that the mind (acting via the central nervous system's adrenaline) overrides the body (acting via the local histamine signal)****.*

The power of the mind to heal the body is entirely dependent on the various physical mechanisms just described. If there is no chemical messenger to act as a go-between, the brain is powerless to alter the action of the immune system. Even when such molecules do exist, they cannot give the immune system supernatural powers. All they can do is tell the immune system to behave in one way rather than another. If something is beyond the immune system altogether, no amount of chemical messengers secreted by the brain will change this.

THERE ARE MANY WAYS THE BRAIN CAN POTENTIALLY HEAL THE BODY. Rather than attempting to cover every conceivable avenue by which the mind might heal the body, from hypnosis to meditation, I have chosen to focus on one particular brain phenomenon – **THE PLACEBO EFFECT.**

THE HISTORY OF THE PLACEBO

IF YOU SEARCH THE TERM "PLACEBO" ON THE ONLINE MEDICAL WEBSITE, PUBMED, YOU RETRIEVE OVER 160,199 CITATIONS. A SEARCH USING GOOGLE, REVEALED MORE THAN 44 MILLION LINKS! To say that this book offers a systematic review of all placebo research would be a stretch. Nevertheless, the material gathered here provides a solid overview of placebo research, and is more than enough to provide a convincing argument that the Placebo Effect is a real phenomenon, and that it can be utilized as a tool to promote healing and good health.

Placebos (from the Latin, "I shall please") are a commonly used practice in medical research and medicine. Dr. W. Grant Thompson describes in his book, **The Placebo Effect and Health**, that the meaning of the placebo has undergone a long and rather tumultuous evolution starting with the emergence of the placebo concept in medieval times to its rather ambivalent meaning today. In 1785, a medical dictionary described placebo as "a common place method of medicine." By 1811, it was a medicine "given more to please than benefit the patient." **WITHIN THE SHORT SPAN OF 26 YEARS, THE PLACEBO WENT FROM A "METHOD OF MEDICINE" TO HOLDING THE FAR MORE DUBIOUS STATUS OF BEING "PLEASING" TO THE PATIENT, AS OPPOSED TO A VIABLE MEDICAL TREATMENT.** Later definitions speak about gratifying, soothing and/or humoring a patient. Today, placebo takes on new dimensions in terms of its psychological effects and the deceptive techniques used in its application. According to Wikipedia, a placebo "is a simulated or otherwise medically ineffectual treatment for a disease or other medical condition intended to deceive the recipient."

WHAT IS A PLACEBO?

Basically, a placebo is an inert tablet, injection, or other treatment that serves as a "dummy pill" or "sugar pill," **WHICH SHOULD BRING NO**

MEDICALLY RECOGNIZED THERAPEUTIC VALUE. The primary purpose behind the use of placebos is to allow medical researchers to test the efficacy of new drugs and other treatments by giving the active drug/treatment to one group, and comparing the results to a "control group," who are only given placebos. To make this work, the control group is deliberately deceived and told they are receiving a particular course of treatment, when in fact, they are just being given a "decoy drug" or "sugar pill." Then, medical researchers compare the results from both groups to see how well their active drug or treatment worked as opposed to offering no real treatment (i.e., the placebo).

Surprisingly, more often than not, control groups report actual or perceived improvement in their symptoms, even though pill or treatment they received had **NO THERAPEUTIC VALUE WHATSOEVER!** In other words, "sugar pill" placebos often lead to the same (and, on occasion, even better) results than the actual drug or treatment being tested. **IT APPEARS IN MANY CASES, IF A PATIENT BELIEVES A TREATMENT WILL IMPROVE HIS/HER CONDITION, THIS BELIEF CAN PRODUCE THE SUBJECTIVE PERCEPTION OF A THERAPEUTIC EFFECT (I.E., THE PATIENT FEELS THAT HIS/HER CONDITION HAS IMPROVED).** Often there is even actual physiological improvement in their condition. This is called the "Placebo Effect."

The Placebo Effect has frequently been discounted by the medical community as simply a psychological phenomenon. People are told that a pill, injection or other treatment is helping them, so their minds "tell" them they are feeling better. This, in and of itself, can be a powerful phenomenon. Think about it. If your brain is convinced you should feel better, you perceive that you are. However, more and more studies are showing that placebos do more than just plant a suggestion that we feel better. **PLACEBOS ACTUALLY CAUSE THE BRAIN TO TELL THE BODY TO HEAL ITSELF, AND IN MANY CASES, THE BODY REACTS ACCORDINGLY.**

> Positive or negative thinking is the decisive factor in any treatment; in many cases, even more important than the medical intervention itself!

THREE CATEGORIES OF PLACEBO THERAPY

Category	Example	Characteristics
Prescription of inert or inactive treatment	• Sugar or dummy pill	• Healer aware • Patient deceived • "Paternalistic"
Inadequate dose or Inappropriate use "Impure" placebos	• Homeopathy • Low-dose antispasmodics • Vitamins for bodybuilding	• Healer may or may not be aware • Patient deceived
Treatment erroneously believed to be effective	• Many "alternative" treatments • Antibiotics for colds	• Both healer and patient deceived

CATEGORIZING PLACEBOS

Arthur K. Shapiro and Elaine Shapiro in their book, **The Powerful Placebo**, outline three main categories of placebo therapy (see table). The first is the deliberate use of inert substances or procedures to treat an illness. Within living memory, physicians, pharmacists and others maintain a supply of inert pills to give patients who seem to require some treatment when a "real" therapy was unavailable or unnecessary. **THIS PRACTICE IS NOW DEEMED PATERNALISTIC, EVEN DECEITFUL**, and many physicians say it is seldom, if ever, employed.

A more common place placebo category is the use of inappropriate drugs or ineffective dosages of drugs. The latter is characteristic of homeopathy. Sometimes, doctors consciously or unconsciously use "harmless" doses of drugs as pacifiers. Examples are the use of anticholinergic drugs for gut "spasm" in doses that avoid side effects (indeed any effect), or the too-late use of antihistamines during an asthma attack. Inappropriate use of drugs includes the employment of vitamins for other than nutrition purposes, such as bodybuilding or cold prevention. Another might be the prescription of antibiotics (used against bacteria) for viral infection such as a cold. The Shapiros delicately called such treatments active or impure placebos.

BY FAR THE MOST COMMON CATEGORY OF PLACEBO USE IS THE DEPLOYMENT OF TREATMENTS THAT ARE ERRONEOUSLY BELIEVED TO BE EFFECTIVE BY BOTH HEALER AND PATIENT. THIS PRACTICE IS AS OLD AS HEALING ITSELF.

Placebo and the Power of the Mind

In 1957, there was a famous and extremely dramatic case of placebo therapy related to the drug, **Krebiozen**. This new wonder drug offered the promise to be a final solution to the cancer problem. A male patient in the late stages of cancer of the lymph nodes and close to the end of life heard about this new drug. All standard treatments had been exhausted and feeling that he was close to the end of his life, the patient beseeched his doctor, Dr. Bruno Klopfer, who was participating in Krebiozen research, to give him the drug. Persuaded by his patient's hopelessness, Klopfer injected him with Krebiozen, but in his heart of hearts, the physician did not expect the patient to survive more than a few days.

Klopfer then watched in astonishment as the patient began to respond almost immediately. The improvement was nothing short of miraculous. Just a few days after the injection, the patient was out of bed and walking around. Klopfer reported that his tumors had "melted like snowballs on a hot stove." **Ten days after the injection, the patient's tumors decreased in size to the point where they could no longer be detected and the patient left the hospital.**

The patient returned to an almost completely normal life. **When he entered the hospital, the patient needed an oxygen mask to breath. When he left, he was well enough to fly his own plane at 12,000 feet without discomfort.** The patient remained well for about two months, until he read in the newspaper that Krebiozen was not delivering what it promised in terms of cancer therapy.

> The history of medicine, in many ways, is the history of the placebo response.

Almost immediately, the patient relapsed; his tumors returned. In desperation, the patient's doctor resorted to a medically and ethically questionable course of action. Dr. Klopfer told his patient that he has just received the **next generation of the Krebiozen drug**, which had been refined to provide **far more effective results. The new drug was simply distilled water administered by Dr. Klopfer.** Again, the patient experienced a full recovery; no detectable tumors or other cancer symptoms. Not having learned from the last time around, the patient continued reading the newspapers and one day found an article on the final verdict on the improved Krebiozen. The American Medical

Association declared that the drug was found to be totally **INEFFECTIVE. THE PATIENT DIED TWO DAYS LATER!**

While this example is highly dramatic, it serves to illustrate how powerful our mind and our perception can impact our physical health. **OUR BELIEF IS THE STRONGEST MEDICINE WE CAN EVER ACCESS TO HEAL OUR BODIES AND LIVE LONGER AND HEALTHIER LIVES.**

PLACEBOS: THE IPECAC EXAMPLE

In an early (and highly controversial) placebo study conducted in the 1950s, pregnant women suffering from severe morning sickness were told they were being given a new medication to cure their nausea and cramping. They were in fact given **IPECAC, A DRUG OFTEN USED TO INDUCE VOMITING IN PATIENTS WHO HAVE BEEN POISONED.** Ipecac syrup is still used in emergency rooms today to induce vomiting in patients who overdose on harmful substances. **TO THE ASTONISHMENT OF THE RESEARCHERS, INSTEAD OF BECOMING MORE ILL, THE PREGNANT WOMEN CEASED VOMITING ALL TOGETHER.** Despite Ipecac's known effects, the fact that the **WOMEN HAD BEEN TOLD IT WAS A CURE** allowed their brains to override the actual physical effects of the drug.

In a later study conducted in 1973, Stewart Wolf at Cornell Medical Centre found 23 stalwart volunteers who were willing to take ipecac on several occasions. The first two times, Stewart just gave each of the unfortunate volunteers the Ipecac; all were nauseated and most vomited. In seven subsequent sessions, **THE VOLUNTEERS WERE GIVEN A PLACEBO BEFORE TAKING THE IPECAC.** They were told the placebo would negate the impact of the Ipecac, lessening or eliminating the nausea caused by the drug. At some point or another, **ALL OF THE PARTICIPANTS IN THE STUDY HAD A PLACEBO RESPONSE, MEANING THEY DID NOT GET SICK AFTER TAKING THE IPECAC.**

However, it was difficult to predict which participants would react to the placebo and which would not, even over several exposures. While the predictive nature of placebo use proved elusive, Wolf's findings did show that each of the 23 volunteers were susceptible to the placebo effects at least once over the course of the study. **INCIDENTALLY, ONE CAN ONLY WONDER HOW WOLF WAS ABLE TO CONVINCE THE 23 VOLUNTEERS TO GO THROUGH THIS RATHER DISGUSTING EXPERIMENT NOT ONCE, BUT SEVEN ADDITIONAL TIMES!**

Psychological Versus Physiological Impact

But, is the Placebo Effect merely a psychological phenomenon or does it actually have a tangible physical effect?

> The Placebo Effect is dependent not on a drug's effectiveness, but solely on therapeutic intention or **BELIEF** on the part of the patient.

The more we believe in a placebo, the better the results. Placebo studies have shown several interesting factors impacting placebo effectiveness:

- Two placebo pills are more powerful than just one.
- Bigger pills are more powerful than smaller pills.
- Injections are more "effective" than pills.

Color can also play a role in placebo effectiveness. The University of Cincinnati experimented on a group of students telling them that they were going to be given sedatives and stimulants. The students were randomly given pink or blue capsules. Shortly afterwards, over half the students reported symptoms of drowsiness and over one third of them reported feeling more stimulated.

The "stimulated" students **AVERAGED A 61% INCREASE IN PULSE RATE AND 71% INCREASE IN SYSTOLIC BLOOD PRESSURE.** Pulse and blood pressure dropped in the "sedated" students, though to a lesser extent of 5% to 10%. But, of the "sedated" group, **40% REPORTED AN "INCREASE IN SLEEPINESS."** Although they were not told which were which, **THE STUDENTS GIVEN THE PINK CAPSULES SAID THEY EXPECTED TO FEEL STIMULATED WHILE THOSE GIVEN THE BLUE CAPSULES EXPECTED TO FEEL SEDATED. IN BOTH CASES THE CAPSULES WERE INERT.** They were simply placebos, containing nothing that should affect mood or physiology.

Why would these characteristics play a role in placebo effectiveness? Scientists have concluded that it is because they help subjects ***believe*** that the "cure" they are being offered will work. **THE BELIEF IN THE PILL OR INJECTION TRIGGERS THE BRAIN TO MANIFEST THE DESIRED PHYSICAL RESPONSE.**

In 1955, Henry Beecher in his paper, "The Powerful Placebo," attributed about 30% of all therapeutic effects to the placebo. **HOWEVER, SUBSEQUENT STUDIES ESTIMATE THAT 50% TO 80% OF THERAPEUTIC EFFECTS CAN BE ATTRIBUTED TO THE PLACEBO EFFECT. IN A FEW CASES, 100% OF THERAPEUTIC EFFECTS ARE OBTAINED WITH THE PLACEBO EFFECT.** Time and time again, the placebo has proven nearly as effective (sometime even more so) as the medication for which it was supposed to be a control.

Antidepressants Versus Placebos

Irving Kirsch, in his book, **The Emperor's New Drugs**, has studied the placebo effect extensively in regard to antidepressant drugs. In 1995, Kirsch and Guy Sapirstein conducted a meta-analysis* of multiple studies in which placebos has been substituted to treat depression. It is a well-accepted research strategy that allowed Kirsch and Sapirstein to review cumulative data across 38 different clinical trials including more than 3,000 depressed patients. Today, meta-analysis is used for major articles in the most prestigious medical journals.

Kirsch and Sapirstein were not surprised to find that across the trials, patients given a placebo **REPORTED 75% IMPROVEMENT** as compared to those patients who received the real medication. Their initial hypothesis was that there was a powerful placebo effect in the treatment of depression. **HOWEVER, WHAT DID SURPRISE THEM WAS HOW SMALL THE DIFFERENCE WAS BETWEEN THE IMPROVEMENT RESPONSE OF THE DRUG AND THE PLACEBO (CALLED THE DRUG EFFECT).**

To understand the drug effect, first realize that the drug is only one element that might contribute to a patient's improvement. Part of the improvement might be spontaneous (i.e., it might have occurred without any treatment at all). Part of the improvement, even when taking the real medication, is most likely from the placebo effect. **SO, IF YOU SUBTRACT NO TREATMENT (SPONTANEOUS) IMPROVEMENT AND PLACEBO IMPROVEMENT FROM THE IMPROVEMENT REPORTED FROM TAKING THE DRUG, WHAT YOU HAVE LEFT IS THE "DRUG EFFECT."**

When you consider the chart on the following page, you can see that about 25% of patients **REPORTED IMPROVEMENT RECEIVING NO TREATMENT WHATSOEVER!** The placebo produced 75% of the improvement response of the real medication. That means only 25% of the antidepressant benefit was due to the chemical effect of the drug. **IN OTHER WORDS, THE PLACEBO EFFECT WAS TWICE AS LARGE AS THE DRUG EFFECT IN TERMS OF PROVIDING IMPROVEMENT.** Again, this is based on 38 different trials involving over 3,000 subjects.

---

* A meta-analysis is a review of a large number of studies to identify patterns among study results.

Antidepressant Treatment Study Results

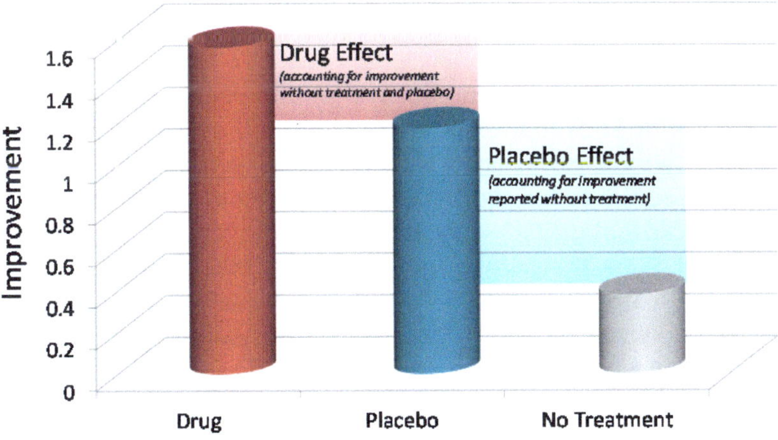

Taken in part from ***The Emperor's New Drugs*** *by Irving Kirsch, Ph.D. (2010)*

IN THE VAST MAJORITY (78%) OF THE CLINICAL TRIALS IN THE META-ANALYSIS, NO SIGNIFICANT DIFFERENCES WERE FOUND BETWEEN THE DRUG AND THE PLACEBO. However, some of the studies utilized what they call an "active placebo." An active placebo is basically an inert drug that mimics the same side effects as the real drug being tested. Active placebos (sometimes called "extra-strength placebos") are used to help negate the effect of patients "figuring out" whether they had been given the placebo or the real drug. By suggesting both the drug and placebo have similar side effects, researchers are able to narrow the drug effect down even more, because patients are more likely to assume they were given the real drug versus the placebo.

Krisch and Sapirstein found that when you compare antidepressant drugs to "extra-strength" placebos, "**DIFFERENCES IN RATES OF IMPROVEMENT ARE NO LONGER STATISTICALLY SIGNIFICANT.**" **THINK ABOUT THAT!** Put more simply, there was no difference between having a patient take the placebo or the drug. The results were the same. **YET, WE SPEND $11 BILLION A YEAR ON ANTI-DEPRESSANTS.**

So, why did having an **ACTIVE PLACEBO** make a difference? The experience of feeling side effects even when taking the placebo helped convince people they had taken the real drug, and therefore they believed even more that it was going to help them.

Kirsch's work substantively questions the efficacy of any drug treatment for depression. The difference between placebo and drug effects are so minimal, who knows what true benefit any drug provides. Patients don't know, and more troubling, physicians do not either. Kirsch puts it best:

> ***Physicians do not systematically prescribe placebos to their patients. Hence they have no way of comparing the effects of the drugs they prescribe to the placebos. When they prescribe a treatment and it works, their natural tendency is to attribute the cure to the treatment. But, there are thousands of treatments that have worked in clinical practice throughout history. Powdered stone worked. So did lizard's blood and crocodile dung, and pig's teeth and dolphin's genitalia and frog's sperm. Patients have been given just about every ingestible – though often indigestible – substance imaginable. They have been purged, puked, poisoned, punctured, cut, cupped, blistered, bled, leached, heated, frozen, sweated, and shocked,*** *AND IF THESE TREATMENTS DID NOT KILL THEM, THEY MAY HAVE MADE THEM BETTER*.

THE PROOF IS IN THE NOCEBO

The antithesis of placebo is ***nocebo***. A nocebo is when an inert or "dummy" treatment is given **AND PEOPLE ARE LED TO BELIEVE THAT IT WILL LEAD TO NEGATIVE EFFECTS**. In a recent study, patients were purposely misinformed that they had been infected by hazardous bacilli and they subsequently underwent treatment. However, there were no bacilli and the treatment that was administered was a placebo. Guess what? Some of the test subjects who were not treated with the placebo medication developed infection-like conditions including fevers, stomach pains, intestinal distress, etc. The mind interpreted the fictional bacilli as hazardous and instructed the body to respond to them as if they were real.

In his book, **Love, Medicine, and Miracles**, Dr. Bernie Siegel reports on a study done in England. This experiment took a group of men and gave them a placebo, telling them it was chemotherapy treatment. Many people generally believe they are going to lose their hair when they go through chemotherapy. Of the men given the placebo, **30% ACTUALLY HAD THEIR HAIR FALL OUT!**

The placebo and nocebo effect are proof positive that perception and how people think are critical factors to physical health. **WHAT WE THINK AND BELIEVE IN OUR MINDS CAN HEAL OUR PHYSICAL BODIES, OR HURT THEM.** With this in mind, consider the potential that a positive mindset and belief system can have on other aspects of your health.

MORE THAN JUST PILLS: THE SURGICAL PLACEBO

In the 1950s, many thousands of people diagnosed with angina pectoris (a decrease in blood flow to the heart muscle) underwent a surgical procedure called ***internal mammary artery ligation***. Based on the work of a surgeon named Davide Feischi who originally developed the procedure in 1939, surgeons would make small incisions on each side of a patient's neck and tie off the mammary arteries that descend down toward either side of the breastbone. Paradoxically, internal mammary ligation involved blocking some of the clogged arteries completely – **THE RATIONALE BEING THAT BLOOD WOULD BE FORCED TO FIND ALTERNATIVE ROUTES BY SPROUTING NEW CHANNELS THROUGH THE HEART MUSCLE.** These new channels would be free of blockages, and so the circulation in the heart would improve – **OR SO THE SURGEONS HOPED.**

Physicians were initially enchanted with this surgery. It was simple, relatively noninvasive, and had few complications. **EARLY REPORTS SHOWED IMPROVEMENT IN THE ANGINA IN UP TO 91% OF CASES AND COMPLETE RELIEF IN UP TO 64%.** Beyond just symptom relief, there were medically measurable effects resulting from the surgery. **ELECTROCARDIOGRAMS ON POST-SURGICAL PATIENTS WERE MORE NORMAL, EXERCISE TOLERANCE INCREASED AND LESS ANTI-ANGINA MEDICATIONS WERE NEEDED.**

However, in 1958, one skeptical surgeon decided to test the validity of internal mammary artery ligation. He conducted the surgery on two of his patients, placing a ligature around each mammary artery, but never tightening the loop. He simply lassoed the artery and left the suture ends loose outside the skin. By not tightening the ligature, no blood was diverted to the heart. The surgeon then observed his patients after the surgery. They experienced great subjective improvement in their angina **DESPITE THE FACT THAT NO REAL CHANGE WAS MADE TO THE BLOOD FLOW TO THEIR HEART.** When the surgeon eventually tightened the ligature using the ends he left outside the skin, **THE PATIENTS REPORTED NO FURTHER IMPROVEMENT.**

That same year, another surgeon, E. G. Dimond, conducted a larger trial of the procedure with eighteen patients, five of which had a sham operation. Of the thirteen who underwent the full procedure, ten of the patients reported improvement in their angina. **ALL FIVE OF THE PEOPLE WHO UNDERWENT THE SHAM SURGERY REPORTED SIMILAR IMPROVEMENTS IN THEIR ABILITY TO EXERCISE AND THE REDUCED NEED FOR MEDICATIONS.**

A year later, in 1959, L.A. Cobb studied seventeen patients whose activity was severely limited by angina. Cobb made skin incisions under local anesthesia, and only after the initial cuts were made, was presented with a card that randomly showed if that patient was to receive the full surgery, or if he should conduct the sham surgery. **AGAIN, THE FINDINGS SHOWED THAT THERE WAS NO DIFFERENCE IN PATIENTS RECEIVING THE ACTUAL SURGERY OR THE SHAM SURGERY. THEY ALL TENDED TO FIND THEIR SYMPTOMS IMPROVED.** Patients across the board improved regardless of whether the surgeon actually did anything after they cut them open or not. One could deduce that the simple act of telling a person that they were going to have surgery, making small incisions in their neck and then closing them up was all that was required to relieve angina. **AFTER MORE THAN 10,000 MAMMARY ARTERY LIGATION OPERATIONS, THIS PROCEDURE WAS ABANDONED IN THE 1960S.**

The results of these studies are significant, but many are fraught with controversy. Back in the 1950s, patients' rights were not as well established as they are today. There are serious ethical questions about surgeons using their patients as guinea pigs to see if a procedure was medically valid or not. Today, patients are told if they are taking part in a placebo study, which tends to skew the data, making it much harder for scientists to determine whether an outcome is medical treatment or placebo related.

KNEE SURGERY IS PLACEBO PROOF POSITIVE

Between 1995 and 1998, a large and well-designed placebo study was conducted by J. Bruce Moseley, M.D. in Houston, TX. An orthopedic surgeon, Moseley has been recognized as one of Houston's leading experts in Orthopedic Sports Medicine for over 20 years, and has served as the team physician for the Houston Rockets, the Houston Comets, and the U.S. Men's and Women's Olympic Basketball "Dream Team." **MOSELEY KNEW THAT MANY PATIENTS REPORTED SYMPTOM RELIEF AFTER ARTHROSCOPIC**

SURGERY FOR OSTEOARTHRITIS OF THE KNEE, BUT NO ONE KNEW ACTUALLY WHAT PART OF THE SURGICAL PROCEDURE PRODUCED THE MOST EFFECTIVE RESULT.

Basically, arthroscopic knee surgery consists of three elements. The first aspect is ***arthroscopy***, the inspection of the knee cavity via a medical imaging devise that is inserted into the knee through three small skin incisions. The second element, ***lavage***, occurs after visual examination of the inside of the knee, when the surgeon then washes/rinses the osteoarthritic joint to remove harmful debris that has accumulated from the degenerative process of osteoarthritis. Finally, the third element, ***débridement***, consists of smoothing out the rough edges of the joint surfaces to permit better function.

Earlier placebo trials had been performed to see if arthroscopic knee surgery was an effective treatment. However, these were not blind studies and it was obvious to the patients whether or not they received the surgery. **SO, MOSELY AND HIS TEAM DESIGNED A FAR MORE STRUCTURED STUDY THAT WAS A RANDOMIZED, DOUBLE-BLIND, CONTROLLED TRIAL ALLOWING VALID ASSESSMENT OF ARTHROSCOPIC KNEE SURGERY.** While patients were told that they were part of study that could potentially involve them having a sham surgery, **MOSELEY AND HIS TEAM WENT TO GREAT LENGTHS TO ENSURE THAT PATIENTS WERE NEVER SURE WHETHER THEY HAD THE REAL OR PLACEBO PROCEDURE.**

Between October 1995 and September 1998, a total of 180 patients from the Houston Veterans Affairs Medical Center with osteoarthritis of the knee were randomly assigned to receive one of three treatments:

Group I: Arthroscopic Lavage – patients in this group received three skin incisions, a diagnostic arthroscopic inspection was conducted, and the joint was lavaged with at least 10 liters of fluid.

Group II: Arthroscopic Débridement – patients in this group received three skin incisions, a diagnostic arthroscopic inspection was conducted, the joint was lavaged with at least 10 liters of fluid, and rough articular cartilage was shaved, any torn or degenerated fragments were trimmed and the remaining meniscus was smoothed to a firm and stable rim.

Group III: Placebo Procedure – patients in this group received three skin incisions and underwent a simulated débridement without insertion of the arthroscopy. In other words, Moseley and his team pretended to do the surgery, going through the motions even though they actually didn't enter the knee cavity.

The placebo procedure, as detailed in the study findings published in *The New England Journal of Medicine* in July 2002, stated:

> ***After the knee was prepped and draped, three 1-cm incisions were made in the skin. The surgeon asked for all instruments and manipulated the knee as if arthroscopy were being performed. Saline was splashed to simulate the sounds of lavage. No instrument entered the portals for arthroscopy. The patient was kept in the operating room for the amount of time required for a débridement. Patients spent the night after the procedure in the hospital and were cared for by nurses who were unaware of the treatment-group assignment.***
>
> "A Controlled Trial of Arthroscopic Surgery for Osteoarthritis of the Knee," J. Bruce Moseley, et. al., *The New England Journal of Medicine*, July 11, 2002 (p. 81-88).

Even in follow-up visits, the patients were never told what treatment group they were in. **However, in each of their follow-up visits (at 2 weeks, 6 weeks, 3 months, 6 months, 12 months, 18 months and 24 months), patients were asked to guess whether they had received the real surgery or the placebo.** Patients in the placebo group were no more likely than patients in the other two groups to guess they had undergone a placebo procedure. For example, at two weeks, 13.8% of the patients in the placebo group guessed that they had undergone a placebo procedure, and 13.2% of the patients in the lavage and débridement groups guessed that they had undergone the placebo procedure.

At each follow up visit, the patient was asked to provide a detailed assessment of their pain and knee function. Moseley and his team devised multiple assessments including self-reporting pain scales where the patient could quantify their own perceptions of the effectiveness of the surgery. More importantly, **an objective functionality scale was used that measured how quickly a patient could walk 30 meters (100 ft) and how long it took them to climb up and down a flight of stairs.** The faster times equated to a higher degree of knee function. **The results of the study were incredible!**

At no point in the study did either of the two arthroscopic-intervention groups have greater pain relief than the placebo group.

In other words, it didn't matter if a patient actually received the surgery or simply had three small incisions made with no other surgical procedure; all patients reported pain-relief to some degree. In fact, at the two-week follow up, the objective walking and stair climbing results were poorer in the débridement group than in the placebo group (i.e., the people who actually had the rough edges of their knee joint smoothed out had more trouble walking and climbing than the people who had no invasive treatment). More importantly, a trend emerged that those who actually received invasive **TREATMENT HAD REDUCED FUNCTIONING OF THE KNEE AFTER TWO YEARS.**

Moseley concluded, "**IF THE EFFICACY OF PLACEBO LAVAGE OR DÉBRIDEMENT IN PATIENTS WITH OSTEOARTHRITIS OF THE KNEE IS NOT BETTER THAN THAT OF THE ACTUAL SURGERY, THE BILLIONS OF DOLLARS SPENT ON SUCH PROCEDURES ANNUAL MIGHT BE PUT TO BETTER USE.**"

In a video documentary called ***Placebo Effect: Cracking the Code***, Bruce Moseley was interviewed about his study. He postulated that given the results of the arthroscopic knee surgery study, it puts many other orthopedic and other surgical procedures into question.

"All of the back pain and neck pain surgeries are very similar. We are treating primarily pain. Most people are fairly desperate, and they strongly believe that the surgery will help them. I am convinced that a large part of the benefit that we do for that is the placebo effect... possibly all."

J. Bruce Moseley, M.D.
Orthopedic Surgeon

Author's Epilogue to Arthroscopic Knee Surgery Study

In the summer of 2012, I gave the keynote address to 400 osteopathic surgeons and staff at a conference in Scottsdale, Arizona. At a conference dinner, there were ten of us at a table when I asked if anyone had heard of Moseley's knee study. Several people at the table responded that they had. I asked them if it was a solid study. The answer was yes, otherwise it would not have been written up in ***The New England Journal of Medicine***. I then asked what the orthopedic community thought of the findings. One orthopedic surgeon responded, "**WE WERE TERRIFIED. WE THOUGHT IT WOULD DRASTICALLY REDUCE THE NUMBER OF PATIENTS SEEKING SURGERY.**" When I asked if it did, the surgeon responded, "**ABSOLUTELY NOT! NOTHING CHANGED.** There have been 650,000 arthroscopic knee surgeries performed each year, each at about $5,000 a pop."

When I returned home from the conference, I did some more research and learned that the surgeon I spoke with was almost exactly correct, except now in 2012, **ABOUT ONE MILLION ARTHROSCOPIC KNEE SURGERIES ARE DONE IN THIS COUNTRY EACH YEAR, COSTING ROUGHLY $7,000 (DEPENDING ON THE REGION OF THE COUNTRY AND WHETHER THE SURGERY IS CONDUCTED AS AN OUTPATIENT PROCEDURE).**

THAT MEANS THAT ARTHROSCOPIC KNEE SURGERY CONTINUES TO REPRESENT $7 BILLION TO THE MEDICAL INDUSTRY EACH YEAR, DESPITE MOSELEY'S FINDINGS THAT THE SURGERY HAS NO REAL VALUE TO THE PATIENT AS COMPARED TO SHAM SURGERY.

It's Not All In Your Head, Is It?

It is not this author's intention to discount the value of surgical intervention. There are many cases where surgery produces dramatic and undoubted benefits, like the resetting of a broken bone or removal of an inflamed appendix. **HOWEVER, SURGERY IS ALSO USED TO RELIEVE SUBJECTIVE SYMPTOMS, SUCH AS PAIN. CONSIDER THE EMOTIONALLY CHARGED PRODUCTION THAT IS SURGERY** – the painfully bright room, the ominous looking equipment and instruments, the masked faces of the surgical staff, the preoperative preparation, the anesthesia, the ritual of giving consent and placing your life in the hands of the surgeon – **ALL PROVIDE AN ENVIRONMENT THAT ACTUALLY PROMOTES A PLACEBO RESPONSE.** It helps people believe that the process will make them heal, and so they do.

Placebos and Pain

As early as the late 1970s, researchers found that by chemically blocking the release of endorphins – the brain's natural pain relievers – the placebo effect could be blocked. This suggested that placebo treatments spurred chemical responses in the brain that are similar to those of active drugs, a theory borne out two decades later by brain-scan technology. Researchers like neuroscientist Fabrizio Benedetti at the University of Turin have since shown that many neurotransmitters are at work—including chemicals that use the same pathways as opium and marijuana. **Studies by other researchers have shown that placebos increase dopamine (a chemical that affects emotions and sensations of pleasure and reward) in the brains of Parkinsons patients, and patients suffering from depression who've been given placebos reveal changes in electrical and metabolic activity in several different regions of the brain.**

"What we 'placebo neuroscientists'...have learned [is] that therapeutic rituals move a lot of molecules in the patient's brain, and these molecules are the very same as those activated by the drugs we give in routine clinical practice," Benedetti wrote in an e-mail. **"In other words, rituals and drugs use the very same biochemical pathways to influence the patient's brain." It's the rituals and treatments that trigger our brains to believe that we can heal that actually allows us to heal.** People **believe** that everything that is being done to/for them in their doctor's office, in their hospital room, and in the operating room is designed to help them heal. That belief contributes a great deal to the level of relief post-operative patients feel. **It is very difficult to separate actual physical benefit from the placebo effect when it comes to many medical treatments.**

The True Value of The Placebo Effect

Belief is the secret ingredient in the placebo effect! **Unlike real drugs, placebos will not help you unless you BELIEVE they will.** For example, you will not relieve your pain unless you believe the "pill" you take is a painkiller.

This is how a placebo works: **you are given a sugar pill (or are injected with an inert solution, or receive a sham surgery) that you believe is a real treatment for what ails you. This causes you to take on a certain belief. This belief triggers your mind to release endorphins, dopamine and other chemicals that allow your body to heal itself, and thereby alleviate your pain.**

Many traditional health professionals tend to dismiss the placebo effect. They wave it aside as a non-phenomenon. Indeed, the term "placebo effect" has taken on a negative connotation even outside the medical field. However, there is a ray of hope, and from all places, the Harvard University School of Medicine.

THE MAGIC BEHIND "FAKE" MEDICINE

Rather than dismissing the placebo like most of the rest of the medical community, **A SMALL GROUP OF PHYSICIANS AND ACADEMICS FROM SEVERAL HARVARD-AFFILIATED HOSPITALS BANDED TOGETHER TO CREATE THE PROGRAM IN PLACEBO STUDIES AND THE THERAPEUTIC ENCOUNTER (PIPS).** Led by Ted Kaptchuk and headquartered at Beth Israel Deaconess Medical Center in Boston, Massachusetts, PiPs is the only multi-disciplinary institute dedicated solely to placebo study. Its purpose is to study not **IF**, but **HOW** placebo effects work. As Kaptchuk states, "The challenge now is to uncover the mechanisms behind the placebo response – what is happening in our bodies and in our brains."

With a degree in Chinese medicine, Kaptchuk is one of few Harvard Medical School faculty with neither a Ph.D. nor M.D. (Kaptchuk's diploma is recognized as a doctorate in many states, but not in Massachusetts). However, his work in the area of the placebo effect has shaken up many "placebo truths" once accepted by the medical community.

For example, in one of Kaptchuk's first randomized clinical drug trials, he gathered 270 subjects who all reported severe arm pain from carpel tunnel syndrome, tendinitis or other chronic pain in the elbow, shoulder and wrist. He divided the subject into two equal groups: **ONE GROUP WAS GIVEN PAIN-RELIEF MEDICATION AND THE OTHER GROUP WAS TREATED USING ACUPUNCTURE.** Each group was warned of potential side effects from their assigned treatment. For the pain-reliever group, they were warned that the pills might make them drowsy or lethargic. For the acupuncture group, the subjects were warned that the needles could cause redness and/or swelling at the puncture sites.

TWO WEEKS INTO THE STUDY, KAPTCHUK WAS STUNNED TO FIND THAT NEARLY A THIRD OF THE SUBJECTS IN HIS STUDY REPORTED SEVERE SIDE EFFECTS FROM THE TREATMENT. In both groups, people started calling in to say their respective side effect symptoms made it so they couldn't get out of bed. The pills made them extremely sluggish, and the needles had caused such inflammation that it was overwhelmingly painful. "The side effects were simply amazing," Kaptchuk stated. However, despite the side effects, many subjects experienced real relief from both the pills, but especially from the acupuncture treatments. **FOR THE FIRST TIME, KAPTCHUK'S STUDY PROVIDED EVIDENCE THAT ACUPUNCTURE PROVIDED MORE RELIEF THAN PAIN RELIEF MEDICATION.**

The problem with all of these results was **THE STUDY WAS A DOUBLE SHAM!** The pills people were given **WERE MADE OUT OF CORNSTARCH**, and the **ACUPUNCTURE NEEDLES WERE RETRACTABLE IMITATIONS THAT NEVER PIERCED THE SKIN**. The study wasn't about which treatment provided a stronger result. It was designed to compare two fake treatments against one another. The findings were definitive: both fakes yielded positive results in managing pain and in **INDUCING PERCEIVED SIDE EFFECTS**.

In another much more scientific study, Kaptchuk collaborated with gastroenterologists to look at the placebo effect on patients with irritable bowel syndrome (IBS), a chronic gastrointestinal disorder that causes considerable pain and constipation in about 15% of the nation's population. This time, the experiment split 262 subjects into three groups: the first group received no treatment, but were told they were on a waiting list to receive treatment, the second group received sham acupuncture treatment, but with very little interaction with the practitioner, and the third group received sham acupuncture, but received a great deal of attention from their practitioner. In Kaptchuk's words, this "very schmaltzy" care included at least 20 minutes of dialogue with the patient including phrases like:

- "I'm so glad to meet you."
- "I know how difficult [your condition] is for you."
- "This treatment has excellent results."

Practitioners were also required to touch the hands or shoulder of members of the third group and spend at least 20 seconds lost in thoughtful silence. **AT THIS POINT, THERE WAS NO SURPRISE THAT THE PEOPLE WHO RECEIVED THE GREATER ATTENTION REPORTED THE MOST IMPROVEMENT TO THEIR IBS, EVEN THOUGH THE ACTUAL TREATMENT THEY RECEIVED WAS FAKE.** At a time when physicians run through patients as if they were on an assembly line, barely taking more than a few minutes with any individual one, Kaptchuk's study is a sobering statement on the chasm that lies between what patients want/need from their health care providers and what they actually receive.

Another area of concern for Kaptchuk was the largest area of criticism for any placebo study: the deliberate deception of the patient or subject as to the type treatment they were receiving. People were being lied to, and the outcry against this ethical component to placebo trials often drowned out the actual findings of the studies. So, Kaptchuk simply decided to take the ethical dilemma out of the equation.

He conducted a pilot study, which was eventually published in the peer-reviewed science and medical journal *PLOS ONE*, where he once again drew subjects with IBS symptoms. This time, one group received no treatment. The other group where told they would be taking fake, inert, placebo drugs. **THE DRUGS WERE GIVEN TO THEM IN BOTTLES LABELED "PLACEBO PILLS."** The only caveat for the placebo subjects was that they were told that placebo drugs can often have a healing effect on their symptoms.

The results astounded even Kaptchuk and his team.

Even patients who KNEW they were taking placebos reported twice as much symptom relief as the no-treatment group.

THESE PLACEBO RESULTS ARE COMPARABLE TO TRIALS FOR REAL IBS DRUGS. A 50% improvement in symptom relief for a real drug would be considered a highly favorable result within the medical community. To have half a study's patients report they felt improvement from a pill that they KNEW to be a placebo, was staggering.

It all comes down to belief, whether it is belief in a drug or other medical treatment, or the belief that even a placebo can help relieve pain and other physical symptoms. **IT IS THE BELIEF THAT IS THE REAL MEDICINE.** Perhaps instead of speaking of the "placebo effect," **WE SHOULD CALL IT THE "BELIEF EFFECT,"** (i.e., the power of belief to allow our bodies to heal themselves). More specifically, I choose to call it:

The Power of Positive Belief

That is precisely what the rest of this book is about; **HOW THE POWER OF POSITIVE BELIEF CAN IMPROVE YOUR HEALTH AND WELLNESS AND LONGEVITY.**

Part **THREE**

The Power of a Positive Approach to Life

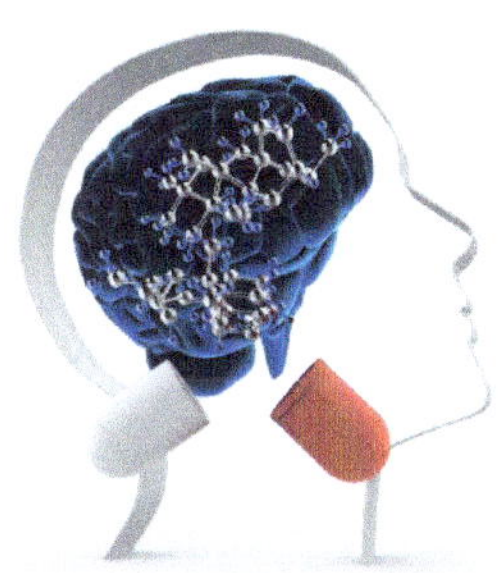

CHAPTER FOUR

POSITIVITY AND LONGEVITY

What would you be willing to do to add ten additional healthy years to your life?

- Would you be willing to run seven miles a day four times a week?
- Would be willing to bike a 120 miles three times a week?
- Would you be willing to eat a vegetarian diet, perhaps even become a vegan?
- Would you be willing to lift weights for one hour three times a week?
- Would you be willing to drink 10 glasses of water a day for the rest of your life?
- Would you be willing to pay $50 a month for a gym membership for the rest of your life?

These are just some of the things people do to improve their health and extend longevity. **UNFORTUNATELY, NONE OF THESE OPTIONS CAN ACTUALLY GUARANTEE YOU THAT YOU WILL LIVE AT LEAST 10 YEARS LONGER.** As a matter of fact, some of the practices listed above can have a deleterious effect on your health (i.e., running and biking and the impact on your knees and hips).

However, there is something you can do that will absolutely extend your life expectancy at least 10 years. You have immediate access to this resource. You can use it 24 hours a day, 7 days a week and 365 days a year. You've probably already guessed if you have read up to this point, **it is harnessing the power of your brain: both your conscious and subconscious mind.**

It is rather interesting when you think about all of the various treatments that people consider for their health, well-being and longevity, that most of us overlook the most potent healing option.

Research Linking A Positive Mindset With Longevity

Many studies have been conducted assessing the impact of positivity on life expectancy.

A Yale University study of 660 elderly people found that those who held positive attitudes **lived an average of 7.5 years longer** than those with negative attitudes.

A Dutch study of 990 people over the age of 65 found that people with positive attitudes **lived on average nearly 9 years longer** than those with pessimistic attitudes. They also found that the positive thinkers had a 77% lower risk of heart disease than the pessimists.

A Mayo Clinic study beginning in the early 1960s that continued over a period of 30 years found that on average optimistic people live 19% longer than pessimistic people. That means if your life expectancy is 80, **you can expect to live an additional 15.2 years.**

A European study conducted by Dr. Ronald Grossarth-Maticek starting in the 1970s, gave a brief paper and pencil test called the ***Pleasure and Well Being Test*** (which is basically a test of whether you have a positive mindset or negative mindset) to over 3,000 people in their mid-fifties in Heidelberg, Germany. Twenty-one years later, he followed up with the same group to get an update of their health status. His findings were incredible:

- Of those who had high pleasure and well-being scores (i.e., positive mindsets) – **75% were alive and well!**
- Of those who had low pleasure and well-being scores (i.e., negative mindsets) – **only 2.5% were still alive!**

Even more interesting was a subset of about 300 people in the experiment who had high scores on the ***Pleasure and Well-Being Test***, but very unhealthy lifestyles. For at least 10 years, these people smoked 20 or more cigarettes a day and drank over 60 grams of alcohol a day. They also had unhealthy diets and did little exercise. In spite of their unhealthy lifestyles, this group outlived a group of healthy lifestyles with low Pleasure and Well-Being test scores by 8.5 years. Healthy lifestyle was defined in this experiment as no smoking or drinking, good diet and at least 1.5 hours of exercise a day. Clearly, a person's mindset has a longevity impact, which is stronger than and goes much deeper than just health habits.

A San Francisco State University study led by Ryan T. Howell in 2007 conducted a meta-analysis review of 24 studies on well-being, health and longevity. They found a 14% longevity difference between individuals with positive mindsets and those with negative mindsets. This 14% difference equated to **A LIFE EXPECTANCY OF MORE THAN 11 EXTRA YEARS!**

There is no question, **THE POWER OF A POSITIVE APPROACH TO LIFE, MORE THAN ANY OTHER FACTOR, INFLUENCES YOUR OVERALL HEALTH AND LONGEVITY**. To put it another way, the mind and your body are linked, and positive belief has a **DRAMATIC IMPACT ON THE FINAL OUTCOME – DEATH**.

So, here is the important question – are you a person whose mindset is positive or negative?

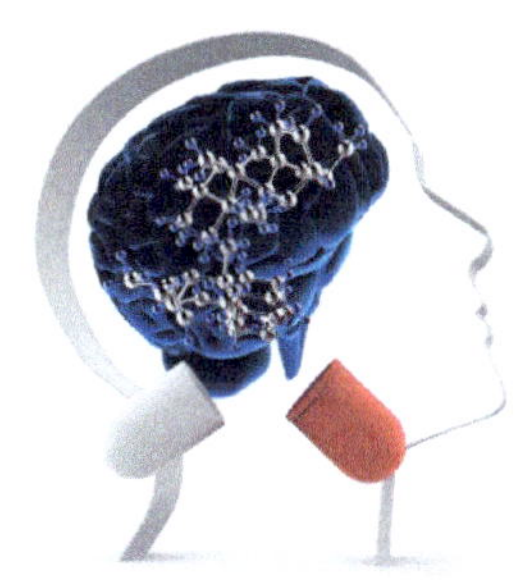

CHAPTER FIVE

ARE YOU POSITIVE?

Are you a positive person or a negative person? Most of us think we are positive people. To be certain you are a positive person, take the following test.

Imagine that you are attending a banquet with 99 other people. You've finished the meal and the banquet is coming to a close. As the toastmaster completes her announcements, she says, "And, now for a special surprise. When you entered the room tonight, each of you shared one of your business cards. The box in front of me contains all 100 hundred cards. I'm going to stir these names up and draw only one. **THE PERSON WHOSE NAME I DRAW WILL RECEIVE A $10,000 CASH PRIZE!**"

You now have two options:

- ☐ Stand up and move toward the podium. The toastmaster is sure to draw your name.
- ☐ Stay in your seat and say to yourself, "It probably won't be me. My chances are only one in a hundred. I never win these things anyway."

If you are like most people, you chose the second option. Realistically, your chances of winning are only one in a hundred. Realistically, you also have absolutely no control over whose name the toast-master will pull from the box.

Since you are now in such a realistic mood, let's offer another scenario.

You are on a cruise and your ship is taken over by pirates. The pirates capture you and 99 of your fellow passengers and hold you hostage in a large room of the ship. It's about lunchtime, and the chief guard strolls into the room. He announces: "I've got some bad news for you. We have enough food for only 99 people. So I've taken all of your passports and put them in this box. I'm going to stir these names up and draw one out. If I draw your name, **WE'RE GOING TO TAKE YOU OUTSIDE AND SHOOT YOU.**"

You now have two options:

- ☐ Stand up and walk to the door. The guard is sure to draw your name.
- ☐ Stay in your seat and think, "It probably won't be me. My chances are only one in a hundred. I never win these things anyway."

The irony in this illustration is that the odds in both situations are identical – one in a hundred. The amount of control we have is the same – none. If you will forgive the pun...

MOST OF US THINK WE WILL GET THE BULLETS AND NOT THE BUCKS.

NEGATIVITY AND THE ANCIENT BRAIN

The human brain developed during a time when staying alive was the first priority for our earliest ancestors. Back in the Pleistocene Era, hominid brains were on constant alert to ensure survival: securing food and water, finding protection from the elements, staying alert for predators and other dangers, etc. Hominid brains were programmed to seek out potential catastrophe at every moment and around every corner.

You might pity our hominid ancestors and their "catastrophic brain," but their programming was the key to our successful existence and continuation as a species. And, despite the millions of years that have passed between their existence and our own, **OUR BRAINS STILL CARRY MUCH OF THE SAME CATASTROPHIC WIRING.**

Excellent evidence of this catastrophic wiring is how the media attracts our attention today. Disaster, death, threats to safety and security, all trigger our catastrophic brains to pay attention and we become riveted to what the media presents as the latest potential dangers to our continued existence. Trying to stay positive and happy when we are inundated with these negative messages can be quite a struggle.

Although most people would identify themselves as being "happy" and/or "positive," studies have repeatedly shown a strong tendency toward the opposite.

- We tend to remember failures more vividly than successes.
- We tend to react more strongly to negative stimuli than we do positive.
- We tend to trust negative information more than we do positive.
- Many of us go through our day mostly blind to the good things in life and only pay attention when something goes wrong.

The Six Universal Emotions

Why do we as humans have such a strong tendency toward the negative? Consider the following list established by psychologists as the six universal human emotions.

Four of these emotions (in red) are negative. Surprise is considered neutral as it could be both a positive or negative surprise. **JOY ALONE IS POSITIVE.**

Why do we have so many emotions related to the negative? Psychologists tell us that the ability to focus on negative emotions formed early in the brain's evolution as a result of our ancient danger/recognition system. The purpose behind these elemental emotions are to alert us to potential threats, and to "suggest" a different course of action.

- **FEAR** tells us to run away when danger is near.
- **ANGER** tells us to defend ourselves against aggressors.
- **SADNESS** warns us to be cautious and save energy.
- **DISGUST** urges us to avoid contamination.
- **SURPRISE** (good or bad) immediately heightens our awareness so that we can evaluate a situation.

Only **JOY** does not prompt a response. The pre-frontal cortex, which registers happiness and is used for higher thinking, is an area that evolved later in human development. Joy simply tells us something good has happened and suggests that we do nothing as our current situation is a good one. Unfortunately, however, joy tends to be very short-lived. While negative emotions can persist over long periods of time, we quickly neutralize joy as we become settled into the status quo. Then we switch back to alert mode and become hyper-vigilant again as to how our existence might be threatened.

The Hedonic Treadmill

Our inability to maintain a sense of joy causes humans to be like hamsters on wheels. We go round and round constantly seeking joy in our lives, but only achieve it for a short time before we move on to our next endeavor. **PSYCHOLOGISTS CALL THIS THE "HEDONIC TREADMILL."** We rapidly and inevitably adapt to good things by taking them for granted, and then are forced to seek joy elsewhere. For example:

- The elation over a pay raise soon diminishes and work once again becomes a grind.
- The excitement over getting a new car barely lasts to its first oil change.
- The joy over a new computer or other electronic gadget lasts only as long as the next ad shows us the more powerful and spiffier model available.

The hedonic treadmill can be a never ending exercise, as long as we hold to the **BELIEF** that our happiness is contingent on factors outside of ourselves. **THE TRICK IS TO SHINE THE LIGHT OF AWARENESS ON THE NEGATIVITY IMPULSE WITH WHICH OUR BRAINS ARE INNATELY PROGRAMMED.**

> "**Emotion** travels from person to person like a virus."
>
> Sigal Barsade
> Professor of Management
> Wharton School of Business

Emotions and the Multiplicity Effect

If you agree that negativity is a primary construct for an individual human mind, bring people together in community and you will see the effect increase exponentially. Negativity is contagious and spreads quickly, especially within groups of people. "**We engage in emotional contagion**," states Sigal Barsade, a Wharton management professor who studies the influence of emotions on the workplace. "**Emotions travel from person to person like a virus.**"

But, within this information is our first ray of hope. If negativity is contagious, is it possible that positive emotions are also contagious? Of course, the answer is "Yes!" If we can keep ourselves focused on the positive, then we can serve as an antidote to others' negativity and immunize ourselves against further negative contamination.

But, how do we actually break away from our instinctive negative tendencies and seek out the positive in life? Can our brains actually learn to "rewire" themselves toward the positive?

Rewiring the Brain & Neuroplasticity

Recent scientific studies have shown that the brain can actually physically rewire itself. **Neuroplasticity refers to the changes that occur as the brain reorganizes itself as a result of new thought(s) or behavior(s).**

For example, a new therapy has been shown to improve function in stroke patients. Traditional therapy methods have patients compensate for their diminished capacity in one arm by learning how to use their still strong arm to accomplish the daily tasks of both arms. **Constraint therapy, however, takes the opposite approach.** It requires that a patient's strong arm be "constrained" (in a sling), forcing the stroke-affected arm to complete common tasks.

The results of this new therapy have been very positive. Not only have patients been able to regain more use of their stroke-affected arm, **BUT STUDIES HAVE SHOWN THAT SOME AREAS OF THEIR BRAIN NORMALLY USED FOR OTHER FUNCTIONS WERE "RECRUITED" TO HELP MOVE THE AFFECTED ARM.** MRI scans clearly showed activity in brain areas that were not active at the start of the therapy. The brain actually physically rewired itself! No matter what our age, we can rewire our neural pathways through our actions and thoughts.

We can rewire our "negative" mindsets into positive ones. In order to understand how, we will look at how the brain actually works.

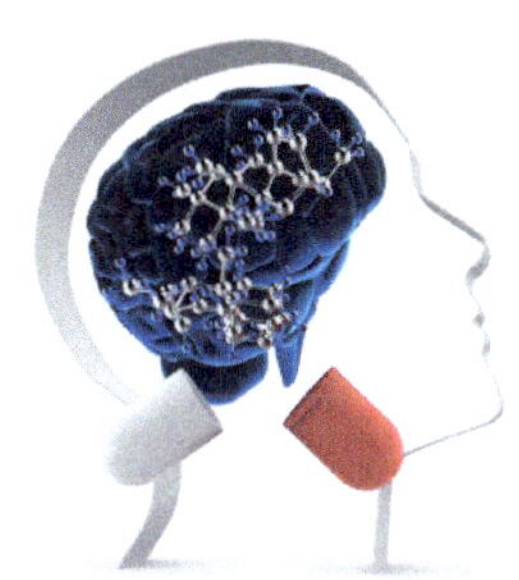

Chapter Six

How the Brain Works

Think about everything you do in a day. It's a pretty long list. You might start by swinging your legs out of bed, standing up and then you possibly... shower, dress, walk, talk, cook, eat, clean, drive, dial, read, write, start, stop, and possibly even program the DVR. How is it that you know how to do all of these things? Most likely, it's because you have done them before.

Now, imagine if, from the time you go to bed tonight to the time you wake up tomorrow, you forgot how to do any and all of the things we listed earlier... that you had to start tomorrow without any memory from the previous day (or any of the days before that). You would have to learn how to do the simplest things from the beginning. Think of just how little we all would accomplish in our lives if we had to start from scratch each day. Take driving your car for example. If you forgot all of what you do "automatically" without conscious thought when you drive and had to consciously think through every driving behavior, you would arrive at work just in time to begin your drive home at the end of the day.

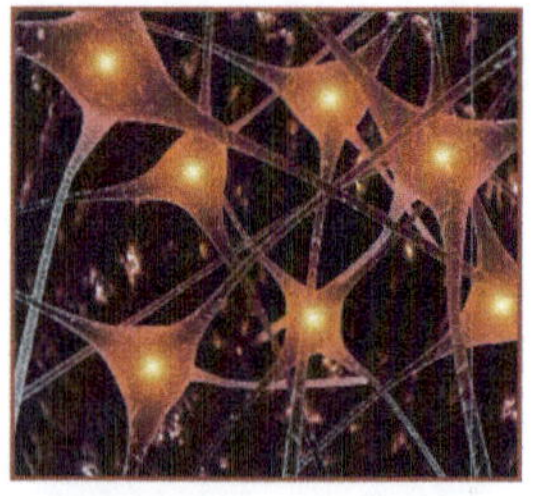

Thankfully, our brains make sure we don't have to do this. They are incredible mechanisms for connecting and storing information. The underlying function of the brain is to make connections and associations by linking bits of information to one another and then storing them for later use. These connections and associations are made via very complex chemical and physical processes.

- The brain has around one billion neurons.
- Each neuron can have up to 100,000 dendrites and one axon. Think of a neuron as a tree with one trunk (the axon) and lots of roots (the dendrites).
- The connections between our neurons, connected by the dendrites, are the "wiring" that guides our thoughts, behaviors and actions.

Scientists tell us there are actually more possible ways to connect the brain's neurons than there are atoms in the entire universe.

THROUGH EXPERIENCE AND PRACTICE WE GAIN MANY LEVELS OF "KNOWLEDGE" THAT BECOME "WIRED" OR "PROGRAMMED" INTO OUR BRAINS. Our brains are vigilant in their attempt to hardwire everything they can. Once information is "wired" or programmed into our brains, we often don't have to think about it anymore. But, while our wiring can help us get through the day, it also limits us by promoting unconscious assumptions. We do not always think things through and just go through our days on automatic.

As you read this right now, you are probably filtering out several things around you... people talking, the feel of the clothes against your body, the flow of air through your nostrils as you breathe in and out. You could never focus on reading if you didn't limit your awareness to exclude other things going on in and around you.

So, the fact that we all walk around with mental limitations as to how we think and what we do is very natural. It's a protective process to help us deal with everyday life. However, the same wiring that helps protect us can also close us in by not letting us see what else might be out there.

There you sit reading this book and without knowing it, a friend of yours comes behind you and taps you on the shoulder. You jump out of your seat. Your brain, for the moment being focused on the text on this page, didn't let you sense your friend's approach. The same thing can happen on a much larger scale.

The Power Of Negative Limitations

Can you run a four-minute mile? Probably not. Most people can't. Being able to run that fast probably isn't very important to you. However, for some people, being able to run a four-minute mile is at the top of their lifetime achievement list. Since the time of the ancient Greeks, running fast has been a highly prized ability. The Greeks tried lots of ways to get people to run faster – even having lions chase runners in order to make them run faster! Not too surprisingly, the lions often won, making running a rather hazardous profession in ancient Greece.

Even now, the spectacle of runners racing around a track can make hearts pound all over the world. The question of who really is the fastest human being on Earth is an enticing one. Over the years, one track and field event has captured the special fascination of spectators: the one-mile race.

At one point in the late 1800's, when the world record for the one-mile race was around 4 minutes and 15 seconds, speculation began as to who would break the four-minute mile. For decades, runners trained, strained and stretched themselves to the utmost to break that four-minute barrier, with no avail.

People started to believe that humans weren't physically capable of running that fast. Experts testified that anatomically, our bone structure and lung capacity weren't up to the task. These so-called limitations, plus numerous other human physical shortcomings, all seemed to conspire to make the four-minute mile an unreachable goal. Many runners came within a gnat's eyelash of achieving the impossible, but all of them failed, and the legend of the achievement's impossibility mushroomed. The runner's mindsets "told" them that a mile could not be run in under four minutes. It even took on a title: "**The Four-Minute Barrier.**" That's how people saw it. It was a great wall that you could come close to touching, but could never break through.

Everything changed on May 6, 1954, when 25-year-old British runner, Roger Bannister, crashed through the barrier and ran the mile in 3:59:4 minutes at Oxford. People worldwide were stunned, convinced that it had to be a fluke or a miracle. Well, whatever it was, it soon reached epidemic proportions. **The same year that Bannister crashed through the barrier, so did 37 other runners! The following year, more than 300 runners ran a mile in less than four minutes.**

Think about this for a minute. For hundreds of years, no one could run a four-minute mile. Then, after one person did, more than 350 other people were able to do the same thing within the next 18 months. What happened? Did humanity suddenly take a huge evolutionary leap forward in 1954? No, probably not. However, the way people **thought** about the four-minute barrier took a huge leap. In this case, Roger Bannister caused people to **change their relationship** with their **BELIEFS** about the four-minute mile.

Roger Bannister's feat (pun intended) allowed runners all over the world to expand their perspective. Once they started to believe that a four-minute mile was within their grasp, they began to run faster. Why? Because their brains now thought of a four minute mile as something they could actually do... so they just did it. And the momentum hasn't stopped yet. The current world record for the mile is 3:43:13 minutes.

> Most world class athletes will tell you the mind must first believe before the body can achieve.

Perception: Blinding the Mind's Eye

Our perceptions are our reality. The beliefs we have wired into our brains determine what we see, how we see it and how we choose to react to that information. And, while our beliefs can be helpful to us, they sometimes limit our perceptions by actually fooling the brain into "thinking" things that aren't true or real. For example, take a moment to focus on the image below. Do you see dots flashing all over the grid? The fact is there are no dots. It is simply an optical illusion that is designed to "fool" your brain into perceiving moving and/or flashing dots.

We can get into trouble when our beliefs get in the way of dealing with new information or situations. Let's look at how.

- The Brain Misinterprets Information
- The Brain Adds In Information
- The Brain Edits Out Information
- The Brain Arranges Information to Meet Expectations

The Brain Misinterprets Information

Sometimes the brain takes information and misinterprets it because the information is similar to something already programmed into its matrix. For example, imagine you are driving up a narrow mountain road late one evening. Up ahead, you see a single headlight coming toward you. Your brain takes in the information of a single headlight and quickly interprets it as a motorcycle. You decide to continue forward around a sharp turn because you know there is enough room on the road for both your vehicle and the motorcycle.

So far, so good? Not really. Up until now, you have only relied on your existing wiring to determine your actions and reactions. But, what if you were to switch out of your pre-wired mode and actually took a moment of self-awareness, to see that the single headlight wasn't a Harley or a Vespa... but, an eighteen-wheel truck with **ONE HEADLIGHT OUT**? The possibility of that option wouldn't have crossed your mind if you didn't actually **THINK** about it. But, if you did, it certainly would affect your actions (not to mention your heart rate).

The brain, by its very nature, can misinterpret information, especially if that information is similar to something already pre-wired into our thinking.

The Brain Adds In Information

Sometimes our brain causes us to add in information that, in actuality, isn't there. For example, what do you see below?

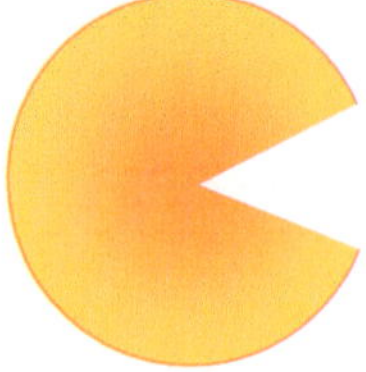

Most people would respond with something like "a pie with a slice taken out of it" or perhaps "a Pacman." Now, consider the next image. What do you see now?

Do you see three "Pacmen?" So far, so good. Now it gets a little more complicated. What do you see on the following page?

Do you see five Pacmen... or do you see a five-pointed star? If you see a star, you are wrong. There is no star. There is just empty space between five colored shapes. Your brain "added in" a star because it recognized a pattern that it already had wired into it from past experience. In fact, the ability for the brain to add in information is so strong that, for some people, the "star" actually appears whiter and brighter than the rest of the paper outside the "star." But, all you are actually "seeing" is five "Pacmen" arranged in a circle.

The Brain Edits Out Information

Sometimes, the brain edits out new information because it doesn't fit into an existing pattern/relationship. By way of an example, read the words below out loud. Ready? Go.

What did you say? Was it "When you wish upon a star?" If you think so, check again. Keep checking until your brain "sees" what it most likely previously omitted. **Have you found the second "a"?** Most of us are wired so that we don't see the second "a" in the image. We edit it out as if it weren't there, and we do this all the time with information coming into our brains without ever realizing it. It is very easy to miss important information because of it.

The Brain Arranges Information to Meet Expectations

Sometimes, the brain takes new information and shuffles it around to fit into a pattern we are familiar with. For example, can you make out the sentence below?

We mkae sesne of waht we "pierceve" oistude of orusevlses in lgrae prat baesd on the pearttns of wniirg we hvae inidse our midns.†

This interesting phenomenon was reportedly first discovered in a study at Cambridge University and has become known as **Typoglycemia**. According to the study, people can read perfectly any text as long as the **first** and the **last** letters maintain their respectful positions. It doesn't matter if all the other letters in the word are mixed up, as long as the first and last letters are in the right place, **pattern recognition in the brain allows us to "read" the word correctly**.

You see, the brain has been programmed to recognize most of the words we read without actually needing to process every letter. It recognizes the pattern of words by their "frame" of the first and last letter, and by the basic length of the word. The middle letters, whatever their order, aren't as important to our recognition ability as the first and last letters. The first and last letters tell us what we should expect to see... the brain **rearranges** the rest according to existing patterns.

Now, if the brain can do this within the relatively simple process of reading, **thnik** about how your brain might be rearranging other new and far more important information to meet its pre-programmed expectations (say about your health and wellness). The brain's ability to add in information, edit out information, and rearrange information, results in what is called **Cognitive Consistency Syndrome**.

---

† Here is the unscrambled version of the sentence above. "We make sense of what we "perceive" outside of ourselves in large part based on the patterns of wiring we have inside our minds."

MISBELIEFS ABOUT AGING

One of the greatest misbeliefs in the world today is about aging and its inescapable effect on the human body. There is a global belief that as we get older, our bone density will decrease, our muscles will weaken, our eyesight and hearing will deteriorate, we will become incontinent, suffer cognitive loss, etc. and on and on.

However, what if many of our beliefs about aging are untrue. Remember, our beliefs can have actual physical effects (go back to the chapter on Placebos if you need proof). What if all we need to do to reverse aging is access that part of the brain that tells us it is inevitable? What if the antidote to aging is simply changing what we believe about its effects and consequences?

Consider, **FAUJA SINGH**, *a British centenarian marathon runner of Punjabi Sikh descent. He was born on April 1, 1911 and is 101 years old. He is also the current world record marathon holder in his age bracket. His current personal best time for the London Marathon (2003) is 6 hours 2 minutes, and his marathon record, for age 90-plus, is 5 hours 40 minutes, which he earned at the age of 92, at the 2003 Toronto Waterfront Marathon.*

In October 2011, Singh became the first 100-year-old to finish a marathon, completing the Toronto Waterfront Marathon in 8:11:06. Singh has stated that he will retire from competitive running after he takes part in the Hong Kong marathon on February 24, 2013 (just 5 weeks shy of his 102nd birthday), but he fully intends to continue running for pleasure.

Then there is **ERNESTINE "ERNIE" SHEPHERD**, *who at age 75, is a personal trainer, professional model, and competitive bodybuilder. She also self-reports that she is happier and more fulfilled than she's ever been in her life. Shepard had been a model in Baltimore for years, but at age 56, she and her sister Mildred Blackwell went to try on swimsuits and found their bodies were out of shape. They started taking aerobics classes.*

Her sister began competing in bodybuilding shows under the name Velvet, and Ernestine followed under the name Ernie. Sadly, Ernie's sister died in 1992 of a brain aneurysm. Rather

than let her sister's death detract her, Ernie carried on her bodybuilding career in honor of her sister's achievements. Since age 56, Ernie has won two bodybuilding titles, as well as run nine marathons. She runs about 80 miles a week, and does not take supplements. In March of 2010, on stage in Rome, Italy, this grandmother was officially given the title of World's Oldest Performing Female Body Builder by Guinness World Records.

Finally, there is 70 year old, **ANNETTE LARKINS**, *who is known as the "Ageless Beauty." Annette has become a sensation as a bombshell whose body, skin, energy and vitality completely contradict her biological age.*

The jaded have accused Annette of simply having good genes. But, this grandmother and self-help author says if all she did was follow her genetic programming, she would have been in the ground before age 50. Both Annette's mother and grandmother died of breast cancer very early in life and diabetes runs rampant up and down her family line.

Larkins herself is a diabetic, and while she takes diabetes and heart medication, she also chooses a healthy positive lifestyle. In a 2012 interview, Larkins stated that she doesn't even remember the last time she had a cold or took so much as an aspirin. But the diplomatic woman, who speaks three languages and sharpens her mind on her library of 5,000 books, acknowledges that when it comes to health and vitality, it's how you choose to live, **AND WHAT YOU CHOOSE TO BELIEVE**, *that makes all the difference.*

FAUJA SINGH, **ERNIE SHEPARD** *and* **ANNETTE LARKINS** *are proof positive that aging is merely a state of mind: a program we have wired into our brain. They do not believe that mobility, strength and beauty must all be sacrificed by the march of time. Their beliefs allow them to break down the perceived barriers of aging, and achieve heights others find impossible. But, why it is so hard to change our mindsets about aging (or anything else)? What keeps us from simply changing our beliefs and achieving whatever we desire?*

Cognitive Consistency Syndrome

All of us selectively process information by **READILY ACCEPTING WHAT CONFIRMS/CONFORMS TO OUR CURRENT BELIEFS/EXPECTATIONS AND SYSTEMATICALLY IGNORE OR DISTORT INFORMATION THAT IS CONTRARY TO OUR BELIEFS/EXPECTATIONS.**

Cognitive Consistency Syndrome (CCS) is a tendency for people to seek out and/or interpret information that confirms their preconceptions or beliefs, independently of whether the information is true. People reinforce their existing attitudes by selectively collecting new evidence, by interpreting evidence in a biased way, or by ignoring the information altogether. **All of us tend to test our beliefs in a one-sided way, focusing on one possibility and frequently failing to examine alternatives.**

Cognitive Consistency Syndrome can lead to disastrous decision-making, especially in regard to our health. Consider the many health fads that have come and gone in recent years – diet pills that caused heart issues, abdominal strengthening devices that cause serious spinal injuries, etc. We all have beliefs about what is good for us and what isn't. But, what if our beliefs aren't true? What if what we believe is doing us more harm than good?

> Cognitive Consistency Syndrome contributes to over-confidence in existing personal beliefs and an unwillingness or, at times, an inability to view information with any kind of real objectivity.

If you have a negative mindset, your brain will seek out negative input and information. If you have a positive mindset, your brain will seek out positive input and information. Now to really understand how the brain works, you must consider the impact of emotions on perception.

Emotions & Their Impact On How The Brain Processes Information

You have learned the brain can misinterpret and distort even relatively simple information because of how it is wired. But, there is one more element to this equation that can greatly amplify these distortions. It is when **EMOTIONS** become added to the mix.

Consider the following four questions:

QUESTION 1: **HOW MANY PEOPLE IN THE UNITED STATES DIE EACH YEAR OF SKIN CANCER?** Approximately 9,600 – yet many of us continue to sunbathe.

QUESTION 2: **HOW MANY PEOPLE IN THE UNITED STATES DIE EACH YEAR IN AUTO ACCIDENTS?** Approximately 38,000 (with 3,189,000 people injured) – yet 86% of the population that is 15 years and older have driver's licenses.

QUESTION 3: **HOW MANY PEOPLE IN THE UNITED STATES DIE EACH YEAR OF DISEASES RELATED TO SMOKING?** More than 430,000 – yet approximately 46.2 million Americans continue to smoke (with 3,000 young people becoming new smokers every day).

QUESTION 4: **HOW MANY SWIMMERS DIE EACH YEAR FROM SHARK ATTACKS WORLDWIDE?** The average for the new millennium is three deaths per year worldwide!

Armed with these statistics, the next time you are near the ocean, walk down to the beach and gingerly step over all the people lying there soaking up the sun's rays and scorching their skin. Wade into the surf until it gets about knee-high. **THEN, AT THE TOP OF YOUR LUNGS, YELL TWO WORDS... "SHARK! SHARK!"** Then stand back and watch people...

- Scramble out of the water
- Stumble over the sunbathers
- Jump into their cars
- Light up a cigarette
- And, drive to "**SAFETY**"

OK, you know you won't actually try this little experiment. But, you get the point. People are susceptible to what we call **"SHARK SYNDROME PERCEPTION."** Despite having a finely tuned capacity for understanding the world around them, people often perceive only what they want to about their surroundings, no matter what the facts are, and despite the efforts of reasonable people to convince them otherwise.

Why? Sharks are scary creatures. They seem much more foreboding than cigarettes or cars. Even though the risk in reality is very small (three deaths per year worldwide), our **EMOTIONAL** reaction galvanizes our perception of sharks. We have a much stronger "emotional" relationship with sharks... even though overexposure to the sun, cars and cigarettes pose a far greater risk to us.

Let's look at this in another way. Which animal potentially frightens you more: a **GREAT WHITE SHARK** or an **ELEPHANT**? Again, despite our earlier clarification about shark deaths, most people would pick the great white.

Why? Because in our childhood, many of us saw movies or read books about loveable elephants like Dumbo and Babar. Either that or we watched in awe as elephants lumbered about doing tricks in circus rings. We have very positive relationships with our "ideas" about elephants.

Yet, **ELEPHANTS KILL AT LEAST 200 PEOPLE EACH YEAR!**

In this case, our positive emotions outweigh the reality of the situation. Because most of elephant-related deaths are in remote areas and receive little to no media coverage, we remain blissfully ignorant of the danger. Elephants are powerful and sometimes volatile creatures, and yet the great white shark is far more feared. If sharks had any legal representation at all, they should have sued the makers of the movie ***Jaws*** for damaging beliefs about sharks forever.

EMOTIONS, DECISION MAKING AND HEALTHCARE

NOWHERE IS THE IMPACT OF EMOTIONS ON OUR PERCEPTIONS AND DECISION-MAKING FELT MORE THAN WHEN IT COMES TO OUR HEALTH. If you have ever had a medical emergency or been diagnosed with a serious illness, then you know the panic associated with this kind of event can be overwhelming. When our survival is at risk, our deepest and most primal instincts are triggered. **CLEAR, DELIBERATE AND REASONABLE DECISION-MAKING BECOMES NEARLY IMPOSSIBLE.**

When you feel ill and/or are in pain, all you want is for those sensations to go away. You don't care how they go away, you just want the pain and discomfort to stop. **YOUR INITIAL INSTINCT IS TO GRASP AT WHATEVER OPTIONS ARE PUT IN FRONT OF YOU.** This is why so many people opt to engage in medical treatments quickly without really knowing exactly what they are getting into. They are in such distress that they will do whatever a physician or other health practitioner tells them to do.

So, are we helpless victims to our emotions and the havoc they play on the rational mind? **YES... FOR ABOUT 90 SECONDS.** In her book, **My Stroke of Insight**, Dr. Jill Bolte Taylor, national spokesperson for the Harvard Brain Tissue Resource Center at McLean Hospital, Belmont, Massachusetts, explains that when an emotional program is triggered in the brain, "**IT TAKES LESS THAN 90 SECONDS FOR ONE OF THESE PROGRAMS TO BE TRIGGERED, SURGE THROUGH OUR BODY AND THEN BE COMPLETELY FLUSHED OUT OF OUR BLOOD STREAMS.**" So, for those 90 seconds or less, our bodies and minds are controlled by the automated responses to a perceived threat. We are controlled by whatever emotion provoked the response, be it anger, fear, shock, etc.

HOWEVER, AFTER THE INITIAL 90 SECONDS, WE HAVE A CHOICE AS TO WHETHER WE STAY IN THAT HEIGHTENED EMOTIONAL AND PHYSICAL STATE. Dr. Taylor, in describing the 90 second rule as it applies to a state of anger, explain this choice as follows:

> ***"If, however, I remain angry after 90 seconds has passed, then it is because I have chosen to let that circuit continue to run. Moment by moment, I make the choice to either hook into my neurocircuitry or allow that reaction to melt away as fleeting physiology."***

In other words, while emotions can trigger a physiological response, that response is fleeting. Even in times of emotional distress, we can regain control not only of our bodies, but our minds. **IT IS A CHOICE, AND THIS CHOICE IS DEPENDENT ON ONE VERY IMPORTANT FACTOR... OUR BELIEFS.**

If we hold negative beliefs, our tendency will be to allow our emotional and mental distress to continue to cycle over and over again. This never ending loop can spiral us down into deep depression and chronic anxiety, making it difficult if not impossible to make rational, conscious choices about our health and well-being.

IF, HOWEVER, WE HAVE A POSITIVE MINDSET AND CHOOSE TO RISE ABOVE OUR INITIAL EMOTIONAL RESPONSES TO FEARFUL SITUATIONS, THEN WE CAN TAKE BACK CONTROL OF OUR CHOICES ABOUT OUR HEALTH AND WELL-BEING. Once again, it is your beliefs that determine your life. They shape your reality. They determine how you act and react to the world.

> ***What we are today comes from our thoughts of yesterday, and our present thoughts build our life of tomorrow. Our life is the creation of our mind."***
>
> Dhammapada
> Ancient Buddhist Scripture

The opening words of the Dhammapada, one of the most revered Buddhist scriptures, articulate an ancient and pervasive idea – the mind is all powerful. In the final part of this book, we offer several Prescription Positive "Scripts" to help become more aware of your beliefs and how you can access your positive beliefs to have a better and longer life.

Part FOUR

YOUR PRESCRIPTION POSITIVE

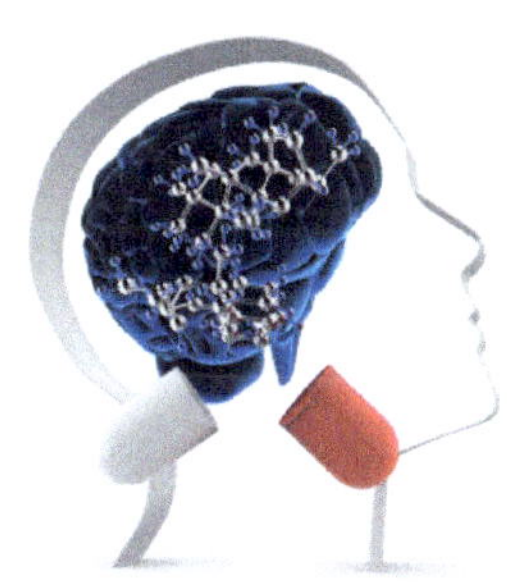

Chapter SEVEN

Prescription Positive "Scripts"

A joyful heart is good medicine,
But a broken spirit dries up the bones.

Proverbs 17:22

How do we fill our Prescription Positive? How do we stop paying so much attention to all of the inadequacy, difficulty and negativity we feel we "must" endure in our lives in order to focus our attention more on the good in life? We focus on our beliefs. When it comes to our health and wellness:

Beliefs are the real medicine.

If we focus on the right things, we can trigger our bodies to stay strong. When we need to, we can also trigger our bodies to heal. Beliefs are so powerful, they literally create our reality. Beliefs are nothing more than agreements about how we choose to perceive reality, and we have the ability to amend, restructure and even cancel those agreements. We have a choice as to what we do or do not believe. However, first we have to be aware of what it is we really do believe. In this final part of the book, we are going to start challenging some of your own beliefs about your life and your health. The following six prescriptions (Rx+ Scripts) can help you leverage the "Belief Effect" and keep a positive mindset no matter what challenges or joys come into your life.

Rx+ Self Accountability SCRIPT 1

Be accountable for your life, especially your health choices. Take positive steps every day to secure a healthy and fully active life.

THE BELIEF:

I AM ACTIVELY TAKING CARE OF MY MIND, BODY AND SPIRIT.

Do you hold yourself accountable for your own health and well-being? Before you say yes, consider the following questions:

- Do you buckle your seat belt every time you are in a car?
- Do you wear a helmet and other safety equipment when you ride your bike or engage in other sports activities?
- Do you stay home, rest, and take care of yourself when you are ill (as opposed to taking medication and going to work)?
- Do you smoke or drink excessively?
- Do you eat a well-balanced diet, maintain a healthy weight, and exercise regularly?

If you answered yes to all of the questions, congratulations! You succeeded in out-maneuvering this author's general and incomplete list of health and wellness measures. However, if you ask yourself if there are ways you can better take care of yourself – and answer honestly – most of us would have to say yes. **RARELY DO WE DO EVERYTHING WE CAN TO ENSURE OUR PEAK HEALTH AND WELLNESS.**

By way of example, this author must admit to his own issue with self-accountability. I am a healthy, active man. I eat well, workout with a personal trainer, and live an enjoyable life both personally and professionally. In 2012, I travelled to Indianapolis on business with a long-standing client. Rising for an early meeting, I was showering in my hotel room when I slipped and fell, banging my head and injuring my back, ribs and hip. I got to my feet, struggled to get out of the tub, and proceeded to follow a full schedule of back to back coaching meetings going well into the early evening. I was in considerable pain from the fall, and it grew worse and worse as the day went on. Finally, returning to the hotel, I purchased some painkillers, and attempted to get some rest before the next round of meetings the following day.

As it happened, my wife was joining me at the tail end of my trip so we could visit family nearby. She arrived to find me at the end of my second day of meetings in a great deal of pain and discomfort. When I asked her to help me put on a back brace that I had picked up at a local drug store, she exclaimed "Dick, you have been working out of a hospital for the last two days! You've met with no less than a dozen physicians since you fell. Why in the world didn't you have yourself checked out?"

Pride, vanity, embarrassment, denial and fear are some of the biggest obstacles to health and wellness. I never did seek traditional medical treatment for my injuries. When I returned home, I saw my chiropractor, who took x-rays to determine that nothing was broken. A few adjustments by him plus a visit to a massage therapist helped with the rest of the healing process. I was lucky. **EACH YEAR MORE THAN 6,000 PEOPLE DIE AND 234,000 PEOPLE ARE INJURED IN HOUSEHOLD FALLS, OVER 80% OF WHICH OCCUR IN BATHROOMS.** For the lack of simple adhesive stickers on the floor of the hotel's shower, I could have become one of those statistics.

All of us must take personal accountability for our health, and in more ways than simply taking safety precautions. Long-term good health comes from taking care of yourself long before a crisis develops. Waiting to do something only after the crisis has arrived is commonly called the "band-aid" approach to health. Sickness is really just the final stages of many missed opportunities to take care of yourself. Sickness is the body's way of telling you that something is very wrong with your lifestyle. In some situations, a simple illness may actually be beneficial in that it forces you to rest and recharge. Your body can only take so much stress and strain before something has to give.

However, there are times when you may need to avail yourself of traditional healthcare. **BUT, EVEN IN CASES WHERE YOU ARE UNDER A PHYSICIAN'S CARE, DO NOT SIMPLY HAND OVER YOUR OWN RESPONSIBILITY FOR YOUR HEALTH.**

Patient-Centered Healthcare: What It Really Means?

We hear a good deal of talk today about patient-centered healthcare. The IOM (Institute of Medicine) defines patient-centered care as "providing care that is respectful of and responsive to individual patient preferences, needs, and values, and ensuring that patient values guide all clinical decisions." In its Declaration on Patient-Centered Healthcare, The International Alliance of Patients' Organizations (IAPO) states that the essence of patient-centered healthcare is that the healthcare system is designed and delivered to address the healthcare needs and preferences of patients so that healthcare is appropriate and cost-effective. The Declaration sets out five principles of patient-centered healthcare:

- Respect
- Choice and empowerment
- Patient involvement in health policy
- Access
- Support and information

What does all of this really mean? It means that even within the healthcare community there is recognition that the patient (i.e., you, me and everyone you know) has been left out of the healthcare process. **The system has gone so far out of whack that patients actually need to have their rights defined and their role within the healthcare process patronizingly spelled out.** It should be self-evident that patients be treated with respect. Of course patients should be empowered to make choices and be involved in health policy, especially as it applies to their own diagnosis and treatment. It should be manifest that patients have access, support and information regarding their healthcare.

> ***Human health is a state of physical, mental and emotional well-being.***

But, unfortunately, our healthcare system has neglected the patient to such an extent that there is now a rallying cry to return to a patient-centered strategy of care. In this day and age, the patient is actually the only one who can be at the center of care. Set aside for a moment that patients are have the most invested in the success or failure of the healthcare, they are also often the only ones who have a complete picture of what is happening.

Specialization has made it nearly impossible for a single physician to know every nuance of how a patient is being treated. In fact, specialization releases them of culpability over the totality of a patient's care. The neurologist focuses on your nerves, the cardiologist on your heart, the nephrologist on your kidneys, the gastroenterologist on your stomach and colon, the dermatologist on your skin, the podiatrist on your feet, and on, and on. Despite all of the detailed record keeping physicians must keep these days, you – the patient – are often the only person involved in your healthcare that actually knows the totality of what is going on.

While the term "patient-centered healthcare" is a signal from the healthcare community that they are recognizing the need to bring the patient back into the healthcare process, it is the contention of this author that the patient needs to be far more active.

> You need to be front and center of your own healthcare experience and take personal ownership for your health and wellness.

Your personal ownership of your health is the true definition of patient-centered healthcare. You have the power and the right to determine your state of health. You also have the power and the right to determine your healthcare experience – how you are treated (both personally and clinically), who you are treated by, etc. Just as importantly, you should have the right to determine whether your treatment is cost-effective, a deliverable that the healthcare industry does not often offer to its customers.

As increasing government control and regulation negatively impact the physician/patient relationship, the responsibility of your healthcare falls more squarely on your shoulders. How you access and leverage your conscious and subconscious mind will become increasingly important to enjoying a long and healthy life.

Making Healthcare Work For You

The fact of the matter is that you must be your own personal advocate when it comes to your medical care. The buck stops with you... not with the physician or other healthcare provider prescribing treatments. The following are suggestions as to how you can take back the reins of your own healthcare experience, and, if the situation ever arises where you can no longer make your own medical decisions, what you should share with your family members about how you wish to be cared for.

Keep Your Own Medical Records: Do you have a copy of your own medical records, or are they in files stored in your physician's office (or multiple physician offices).

In this electronic age, every healthcare provider should be able to provide you with electronic access to all of your medical records, including test results, blood work, x-ray or other images, physician notes, etc. You have the right to copies of all documentation regarding your personal medical treatment. Keep your own medical records, and consider storing them on a computer or other electronic device for easy access in case of an emergency (this author keeps his medical records on a USB thumb drive on his key chain).

It's Your Appointment: When you make an appointment with your physician, they are providing a service for you. It's your time, not theirs, that matters. Take time to prepare for your visit. Think about what you want to get out of your appointment. Write out any questions you might have and don't leave without feeling completely satisfied with how you have been treated (both clinically and personally).

Give Information To Your Doctor: Don't wait to be asked about issues you think are important to your medical treatment. Tell your physician everything he or she needs to know about your health, even things that might make you feel embarrassed or uncomfortable. Do not limit the information you provide to simply the physical. Share how you feel emotionally and mentally, as well. Do not stop until you feel that you have shared every aspect of the concern that caused you to make an appointment in the first place.

Get Information From Your Doctor: Ask questions about anything that concerns you. Keep asking until you understand the answers completely. If you do not, your physician might assume you understand things even when you do not. If it will help you understand something, ask your doctor to draw a picture or show you in an anatomy book where the area of concern is.

Take notes of your visit, or, with your physician's agreement, tape the conversation. Ask your physician to recommend resources like websites, booklets or other materials that will help you understand your disease or condition. Most importantly, ask your physician to list all available

treatment options for your disease or condition, including treatments outside of conventional medicine (i.e., alternative therapies).

Do Not Hesitate To Seek A Second Opinion: If you wish to have a diagnosis verified by another physician, that is your right. In fact, in many cases, your healthcare coverage should include the ability to seek a second opinion. For the most part, physicians will understand that you would like more information before making important decisions about your health (if not, this is a warning sign that you may not be with the right physician). You can even ask for a referral from your current doctor, though you may want to see someone outside their particular practice as physicians who work together often share similar views. Again, make sure you are completely satisfied that you have been diagnosed correctly and have been informed of all your treatment options.

Do Your Own Research And Work With Your Doctor: Inform yourself about your disease or condition. The internet offers unparalleled access to multiple viewpoints on most medical issues. However, be warned that a few hours on the internet does not make you a medical expert. Physicians have dedicated years of their lives to gain the training and expertise to help you. Take the information you have gathered about your condition and work with your physician to develop a treatment plan. Let your physician be your healthcare partner, having them serve as navigator as you steer your own healthcare ship.

Make Your Wishes Known: If the situation should ever arise that you are no longer capable to make your own medical decisions, make sure that you have complete confidence in the person you designate as your healthcare surrogate. Do not just assume that a family member or other surrogate will do what you want them to do.

It is your job to discuss your wishes with them. In the emotionally charged moments when critical health decisions must be made on your behalf, it is irresponsible for you to leave any measure of doubt about your treatment preferences in the minds and hearts of those you love. You are accountable for your healthcare, whether you are capable of making rational decisions or not. If you have not ensured that your healthcare surrogate(s) know what you find acceptable in terms of treatment – and what you don't – you have only yourself to blame.

Ten Important Questions To Ask Your Doctor After A Diagnosis

These 10 basic questions can help you understand your disease or condition, how it might be treated, and what you need to know and do before making treatment decisions.

1. What is the technical name of my disease or condition, and what does it mean in plain English?
2. What is my prognosis (outlook for the future)?
3. How soon do I need to make a decision about treatment?
4. Will I need any additional tests, and if so what kind and when?
5. What are my treatment options?
6. What are the pros and cons of my treatment options?
7. Is there a clinical trial (research study) that is right for me?
8. Now that I have this diagnosis, what changes will need to be made in my daily life?
9. What organizations do you recommend for support and information?
10. What resources (booklets, websites, audiotapes, DVDs, etc.) do you recommend for further information?

Find The Right Physician For You: Make sure that your physician is a good fit for you. Does he/she make the time to speak with you? Does he/she inspire your confidence and make you comfortable. If you do not feel that you and your physician(s) work well together, then it is in your best interest to find others who do.

There is an emerging trend that helps both patients and physicians build stronger and more effective healthcare relationships. Over the years, many physicians have been frustrated by a) the reduction in reimbursement they receive for their services, and b) the fact that this financial situation pushes them into accepting a large number of patients to secure their income.

Many physicians have several thousands of patients under their care, most of which only come once or twice a year when they need something. Overloaded with patients, physicians on average spend less than six minutes with any individual patient, before they move on to the next chart on the door. Physicians don't get to know their patients and vice versa, leading to a very transactional arrangement on both sides.

Concierge Medicine

One solution to this issue has been the advent of **CONCIERGE MEDICINE**. A physician chooses to put a premium on service and patient relationships, but at a cost. Patients agree to pay a fee, which is not covered by insurance, and the flat fee may not cover additional medical charges that might be incurred during an office visit. This fee averages between $1,000 and $5,000 annually, but there are some physicians who charge into the tens of thousands of dollars for their services. Others are starting to offer programs for $250 a year! These are online services, but in the case of one company, they do provide up to six phone consultations with a real physician per year.

To get the best medical treatment for your overall health, try to find a concierge physician certified in both **internal** and **anti-aging** medicine.

Basically, as a patient, you are paying a fee to have your doctor be available to you and for you when you need him/her. You agree to pay extra in order to have your physician guarantee an appointment within 24 hours, and that during that appointment, have your physician really take time to listen to you and understand your concerns and needs. In return, your concierge physician feels less financial pressure and can have fewer patients under his/her care. They also have the time to develop long-term and more fulfilling relationships with their patients. If your budget permits, engaging a concierge physician can significantly enhance your healthcare experience should you need medical intervention or assistance.

Personal Accountability

"**WHAT I REALLY WANT FROM HEALTHCARE IS NOT TO NEED IT.**" Remember that statement from Chapter One. It effectively summarizes the feeling of most people about healthcare. None of us really want to go to the doctor, hospital or other healthcare facility. But, what does it really mean?

Well, the opposite of needing healthcare is having wellness. What more and more people desire is to find ways that will allow them to live longer, more healthful lives without the need for medical intervention. People are always talking about the current healthcare crisis. They go on and on about the increased costs, longer wait times and reduced quality of care.

My own opinion on the subject is that the solution to our current healthcare crisis has nothing to do with Senators, Congressmen or healthcare legislation and regulation. **IT HAS EVERYTHING TO DO WITH PERSONAL RESPONSIBILITY.** By avoiding individual responsibility to one's own health and wellness, people become a part of the problem. **THERE IS NO DOUBT THE HEALTHCARE SYSTEM IS GOING TO HAVE TO CHANGE, BUT SO ARE THE PEOPLE WHO RELY ON IT.** Each of us is going to have to take responsibility for our own healthcare.

The Wellness Continuum

Let's think for a moment about the two ends of the health continuum: illness, wellness, and the contributing factors to each condition.

DEGREE OF SELF ACCOUNTABILITY

More than any other factor, the degree of personal accountability you have for your own wellness and happiness determines how long and how well you live. Most of us do not hold ourselves accountable when it comes to our health and well-being. We eat what we want, as much as we want. We smoke when we want, as much as we want. We drink when we want, as much as we want. We exercise as little or as much as we want, as frequently or infrequently as we want. We sacrifice sleep to our worries and other perceived priorities. We do little to balance the stress we feel in our lives. We allow our immune systems to be compromised, and allow ourselves to fall victim to chronic and totally preventable illness or disease. **THEN, WHEN WE EXPERIENCE HEALTH PROBLEMS, WE EXPECT OUR HEALTHCARE SYSTEM TO "FIX" US AND TAKE CARE OF THE PHYSICAL AND EMOTIONAL PROBLEMS WE HAVE CAUSED AS A RESULT OF OUR CHOSEN LIFESTYLE.**

Consider the following truly troubling statistics about the state of American health.

- Preventable illness makes up approximately 80% of all illness and 90% of all healthcare costs.

- Preventable illnesses account for eight of the nine leading categories of death.
- 75% of all healthcare dollars are spent on patients with one or more chronic conditions, many of which can be prevented, including diabetes, obesity, heart disease, lung disease, high blood pressure, and cancer.

Obesity

It is estimated that 67% of Americans are currently overweight. More pointedly, more than one-third of U.S. adults (35.7%) are actually classified as obese, which puts us at the top of the list compared to most of the rest of the world.

Approximately 17% (or 12.5 million) of children and adolescents aged 2—19 years are obese. Annual medical costs of obesity are as high as $147 billion. On average, obese people have annual medical costs that are $1,429 more than medical costs of normal weight people.

If you are like a whopping 96% of the population, you may not be able to recall the last time you had a salad, since you're one of the hundreds of millions of Americans who rarely eat enough vegetables. And what you do eat, you don't burn off — assuming you're like the 40% of us who get no exercise. Most troubling of all, if you're like any parent of any child anywhere in the world, you may be passing your health habits to your children, which explains why experts fear that the latest generation of American children may be the first ever to have a shorter life span than their parents.

Diabetes

- 25.8 million children and adults in the United States – 8.3% of the population – have diabetes.
- Only 18.8 million people have been diagnosed with the disease (projected to rise to over 30 million people by 2030).
- That leaves 7.0 million people who are undiagnosed.
- 79 million people are projected to be pre-diabetic.

Total costs of diagnosed diabetes in the United States in 2007 came to $174 billion ($116 billion for direct medical costs and $58 billion for indirect costs (disability, work loss, premature mortality).

After adjusting for population age and sex differences, average medical expenditures among people with diagnosed diabetes were 2.3 times higher than what expenditures would be in the absence of diabetes.

The American Diabetes Association has created a Diabetes Cost Calculator that takes the national cost of diabetes data and provides estimates at the state and congressional district level. Factoring in the additional costs of undiagnosed diabetes, prediabetes, and gestational diabetes brings the total cost of diabetes in the United States to more than $220 billion.

Heart Disease

Heart disease is the leading cause of death for both men and women. In 2008, over 616,000 people died of heart disease. Heart disease caused almost 25% of deaths—almost one in every four—in the United States. Below is the percentage of U.S. adults with heart disease risk factors.

Risk Factor	%
Inactivity	53
Obesity	34
High Blood Pressure	32
Cigarette Smoking	21
High Cholesterol	15
Diabetes	11

Approximately 37% of adults reported having two or more of the risk factors listed above. Every year about 785,000 Americans have a first heart attack, and another 470,000 who have already had one or more heart attacks have another attack. In 2010, coronary heart disease alone was projected to cost the United States $108.9 billion. This total includes the cost of health care services, medications, and lost productivity.

Smoking

Tobacco is the leading cause of preventable illness and death in the United States. It causes many different cancers as well as chronic lung diseases, such as emphysema, bronchitis, and heart disease. In 2009, approximately 20.6% of U.S. adults were cigarette smokers. Nearly 20% of high school students smoke cigarettes.

Cigarette smoking causes an estimated 443,000 deaths each year. Lung cancer is the leading cause of cancer death among both men and women in the United States, and 90% of lung cancer deaths

AMONG MEN AND APPROXIMATELY 80% OF LUNG CANCER DEATHS AMONG WOMEN ARE DUE TO SMOKING.

PEOPLE WHO SMOKE ARE UP TO SIX TIMES MORE LIKELY TO SUFFER A HEART ATTACK THAN NONSMOKERS, and the risk increases with the number of cigarettes smoked. Smoking also causes most cases of chronic obstructive lung disease.

HOW TO INSPIRE SELF ACCOUNTABILITY FOR HEALTH AND WELLNESS

True wellness doesn't just come from doing the right things. The choices we make to eat a healthy diet, exercise regularly, refrain from smoking or drinking in excess, etc. all stem from a mindset that cherishes life. Self-accountability for health and wellness finds its root in a belief that life is precious and worthy of living to the fullest every day. **A POSITIVE MINDSET INSPIRES THE ACTIONS THAT WILL KEEP YOU ON THE RIGHT TRACK TO HEALTH AND WELLNESS.**

Whereas many health and wellness experts would provide you with a list of things to do to safeguard your health, these actions/behaviors are secondary to **THE REAL KEY TO WELLNESS: YOUR MIND AND ATTITUDE.**

℞+ SCRIPT 2

Manage Your Stress

Consciously and actively manage the stress in your life. Do what you can to reduce stressors and leverage the stress you have to your advantage.

THE BELIEF:

I AM MORE THAN CAPABLE OF HANDLING ALL ASPECTS OF MY LIFE EASILY AND POSITIVELY.

IT IS ESTIMATED THAT 75% TO 90% OF ALL ILLNESS IS DIRECTLY RELATED TO STRESS. Read that sentence again and realize that one of the most important things you can do for your health is to effectively manage your stress.

What is stress? According to Wikipedia, stress is defined "as an organism's total response to an environmental condition or stimulus." For the purposes of this book, stress is the result of some form of imbalance. We can feel that we have too much of something in our lives, and/or too little of another. Any time we feel something in our lives is out of balance, we feel stress.

There is no question that stress is a prevalent condition in our lives. However, stress is not always a negative condition. We need some stress. In fact, we can thrive on it. Much like the strings of a violin, without a little bit of tension, we don't play at our peak potential. However, in the modern age, we are bombarded with demands and pressures that place incredible stress on us, and this stress in turn, puts enormous strain on our bodies and minds.

A History Lesson

Back in the days when our ancestors lived in caves and we both hunted **AND** were hunted for food, stress often came in the form of physical threats that required us to react quickly and decisively for the sake of our own survival. If we perceived a predator eyeing us hungrily, we didn't stop to "think" about what we should do or how we might be able to escape. We just instinctively switched into **FIGHT OR FLIGHT** mode. **UPWARDS OF 1,400 CHEMICAL REACTIONS WERE TRIGGERED IN OUR BRAINS (MOST NOTABLY ADRENALINE AND CORTISOL)** that caused our heart rates to increase, our digestive systems to shut down, increased the blood flow to the muscles in our limbs, tensed those muscles, heightened our level of sensation, etc. In the end, however, regardless of the outcome of the encounter, we never stayed in that fight or flight state very long. Either the predator got us or we got them. **IF THE LATTER WAS TRUE, THEN ALL SYSTEMS RETURNED TO NORMAL – OUR HEART RATE RETURNED TO NORMAL, OUR STOMACHS CAME BACK ONLINE, ETC.**

Fast forward several thousands of years to today and we still are carrying around much of that same old wiring. We aren't necessarily being physically attacked by predators intent on killing us for food, but we do face situations that trigger our survival instincts all the time. Modern day stresses are more likely to be psychological in origin and prolonged in nature; when our boss confronts us about a problem, when we hear rumors that our organization is considering layoffs, when we have a disagreement with a spouse or child at home. Even though these situations are not immediately life threatening, our survival mechanisms are still triggered all the same. Our heart rates go up, our muscles tense, our senses become more acute, etc.

BUT, UNLIKE AN ATTACK BY A PREDATOR IN ANCIENT TIMES, THESE SITUATIONS OFTEN DO NOT RESOLVE THEMSELVES QUICKLY. We are triggered into fight or flight mode, and then stay in that state for long periods of time. Chemicals continue to be injected into our bloodstream long after a heated, emotional exchange. Our blood pressure can remain elevated indefinitely. When we are under this kind of stress for long periods, it has a wide range of impacts on the body's systems – brain, cardiovascular, digestive, immune, etc. **OVER TIME, THE RESULT CAN BE JUST AS DEADLY AS WHEN A LONG EXTINCT PREDATOR KILLED OFF ONE OF OUR ANCESTORS.**

Homeostasis

In biology, most biochemical processes strive to maintain equilibrium: they keep their systems in balance for optimal functionality. As the human body is basically a large, complex mass of biochemical processes, homeostasis is intended to be our natural, balanced state. The term homeostasis comes from two Greek words, *homeo*, which means "the same," and *stasis*, which means "standing." Some people refer to homeostasis as a state of internal constancy, but homeostasis is not a static state; it is a dynamic and ever changing state that is achieved through a variety of automatic mechanisms that compensate for internal and external changes.

Examples of human homeostasis include our ability to maintain a near constant bodily temperature (98.6° Fahrenheit or 37° Celsius). If external temperatures become too cold, sensors in our skin are triggered to stimulate shivering, a rhythmic contraction of muscles that generates body heat. If external temperatures become too warm, our systems trigger the production of perspiration in order to cool the body. In this way, we are able to maintain a more or less constant internal temperature.

Another instance is in regard to maintaining optimal blood sugar levels in the body. Our cells derive their energy from glucose, and it is vital that glucose levels be tightly regulated. Too much glucose is toxic to cells while too little glucose leads to cell starvation. If the body senses that there is too little glucose in the body, it triggers the release of catabolic hormones (such as glucagon, cortisol and catecholamines) which increase blood glucose. It the body senses there is too much glucose in the body, it releases an anabolic hormone (insulin) to balance out the excess sugar in the blood stream.

Temperature and blood sugar regulation are but two of many automated responses our body has to maintain homeostasis. We are innately designed to be optimally functioning biological machines. Unfortunately for most of us, homeostasis is more of an ideal than a reality. The majority of people live very unbalanced lives, and as result, subject their bodies to a constant battle to maintain homeostasis. **EVERYTHING WE DO EACH DAY EITHER HELPS US TO EITHER STAY IN BALANCE OR PUSHES US FURTHER OFF COURSE.** Our lifestyle choices and most especially our levels of stress influence the degree of homeostasis we have in our bodies. The more stress we have, the harder our bodies have to fight to stay in balance. The more imbalanced we are, the more likely we will create an environment of "dis-ease" in our bodies, resulting in both illness and pain.

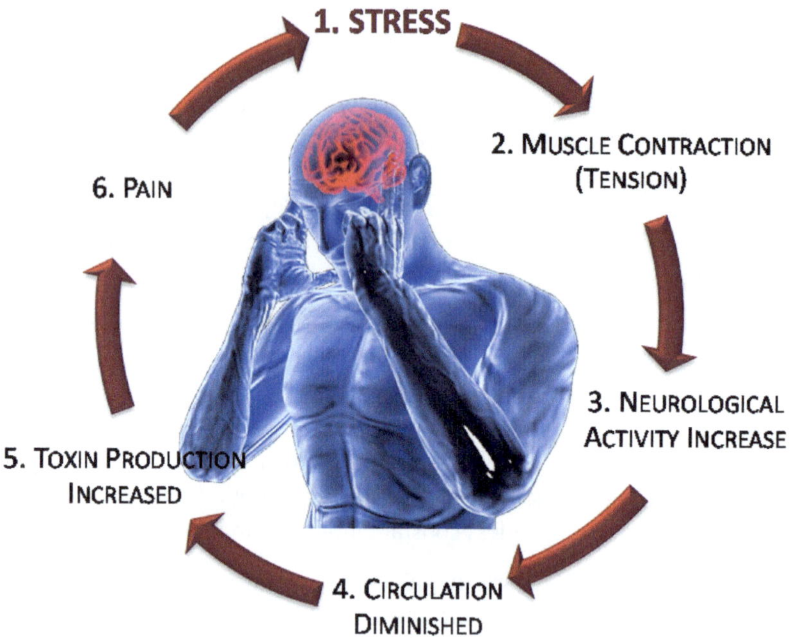

STRESS, TENSION AND PAIN

A normal physical response to stress is to tighten the muscles in our shoulders, jaw, fists and other areas. Staying in a prolonged state of muscle tension due to stress can lead to restricted blood flow to the muscles, eventually leading to pain. If nothing is done to relieve the stress and its resulting physiological effects, the vicious chronic pain cycle comes into effect.

Chronic pain itself creates additional stress, not only due to pain, but also the loss of activity, relationships, job, finances and hobbies. As a result, the more pain someone is in, the more stress they are under. This results in a downward spiraling pain cycle that is difficult to stop.

In addition to muscle tension, stress results in hormonal and neurotransmitter changes in the body, which can contribute to pain. These changes involve biochemicals such as serotonin, endorphins, norepinephrine, dopamine, and, most especially, cortisol.

Inflammatory Responses

Cortisol is called the "stress hormone" because it is a key hormone involved in our stress response. Under short-term stress, cortisol is beneficial and is associated with reduced sensation of pain and improved healing. Under long-term stress, however, abnormal patterns of cortisol secretion can occur affecting the immune system, resulting in increased inflammation in the body.

"Inflammation is partly regulated by the hormone cortisol and when cortisol is not allowed to serve this function, inflammation can get out of control," said Sheldon Cohen, the Robert E. Doherty Professor of Psychology within Carnegie Mellon University's Dietrich College of Humanities and Social Sciences.

A research team led by Cohen found that chronic psychological stress is associated with the body losing its ability to regulate the inflammatory response. Published in the *Proceedings of the National Academy of Sciences*, **THE RESEARCH SHOWS FOR THE FIRST TIME THAT THE EFFECTS OF PSYCHOLOGICAL STRESS ON THE BODY'S ABILITY TO REGULATE INFLAMMATION CAN PROMOTE THE DEVELOPMENT AND PROGRESSION OF DISEASE.**

Cohen argues that prolonged stress alters the effectiveness of cortisol in regulating the inflammatory response because it decreases tissue sensitivity to the hormone.

> Specifically, immune cells become insensitive to cortisol's regulatory effect. In turn, runaway inflammation promotes the development and progression of many diseases, even causing premature aging.

Most people are familiar with inflammation as it applies to injury. If you cut or injure yourself, the wound becomes red and swollen. This inflammation plays a key role in healing because it helps draw blood and nutrients to a wound to facilitate repair of the damaged tissue. But, **INFLAMMATION ALSO OCCURS INSIDE THE BODY, NOT JUST ON THE SURFACE.** While the inflammation in wound healing is limited to the area of injury, chronic internal inflammation can become pervasive in the body, targeting even healthy tissue. **CHRONIC INFLAMMATION PROMOTES DISEASE RATHER THAN HEALING IT.** Inflammation has a hand in most known diseases, most typically heart disease and arthritis. Stress is a key factor in chronic inflammation.

B-R-E-A-T-H-E

The following relaxation exercise is from John M. Kennedy, MD, medical director of preventative cardiology and wellness at Marina del Rey Hospital in California. In his article, *The 15-minute Health Cure,* he outlines his suggested protocol to help his cardiac patients to de-stress.

> *The traditional techniques for reducing stress, such as yoga, are helpful, but typically too complicated and time-consuming for most people. My colleagues and I have developed a simpler approach that anyone can do in about 15 minutes a day. It goes by the acronym B-R-E-A-T-H-E, which stands for Begin, Relax, Envision, Apply, Treat, Heal, and End.*
>
> **BEGIN:** *Pick a time of day when you won't be interrupted for 15 minutes. Find a comfortable location. Many patients use their bedrooms, but any quiet, private place will work.*
>
> **RELAX & BREATHE:** *This phase of the exercise is meant to elicit the relaxation response, a physiological process that reduces stress hormones and slows electrical activity in the brain. It also reduces inflammation. Focus so completely on your breathing that there isn't room in your mind for anything else. Inhale slowly and deeply through your nose. Then exhale just as slowly through your mouth. Each inhalation and exhalation should take about seven seconds.*
>
> *Repeat the breathing cycle seven times. You'll know you're ready to go to the next step when your body is so relaxed that it feels as if all of your weight is supported by the chair or bed rather than your muscles.*
>
> **ENVISION:** *Spend a few minutes imagining that every part of your heart – the arteries, muscles, valves and the electrical system – is strong and healthy. Form a mental picture (it doesn't have to be anatomically accurate) of the heart pumping blood and sending nourishment throughout your body. Hold the mental image for several minutes.*
>
> *Studies using PET scans show that people who imagine they are performing an action activate the same part of the brain that is involved when they actually do that action. Imagining a healthy heart literally can make the heart healthier.*
>
> **APPLY:** *It's up to you when (and how often) you perform this relaxation exercise. Most people can find 15 minutes a day to take a mental break from the stress to keep their hearts healthy. Others also use this technique when they notice that their stress levels are rising.*

During a hectic day at work, for example, you might be able to take a break for 15 minutes to calm down with conscious breathing and visualization.

TREAT AND HEAL: *I encourage patients to embrace the pleasurable aspects of this exercise. Don't consider it a chore. It's more like a spa treatment than a physical workout.*

The healing aspect can be strongly motivating, particularly if you already have a history of heart disease. Every time you do this exercise, you are strengthening the neural networks that connect the heart and brain. This can lead to a decrease in heart arrhythmias (irregularities), an increase in immune-cell activity and even better sleep.

END: *Finish each relaxation session by making a mental checklist of what you have achieved. You have imagined that your heart and arteries are healthy. You have reduced stress hormones, and you are feeling more relaxed and energized than you did before.*

The results are long lasting. People who practice this for a few weeks will find themselves dealing with unexpected stressful events productively and in a calm, focused manner.

Stress and Positive/Negative Mindsets

One of the key ingredients to good health is effective stress management. But, not everyone handles stress in the same way. Once again, it comes down to what we choose to believe about stress that allows us to manage it more effectively. Do you view stress as a positive or do you view it as a negative?

More negative people tend to become overwhelmed by stress, and are far less able to manage stressful circumstances. They tend to assume "victim" mentalities, seeing outside forces aligned against them. They get locked up in a cycle of frustration, even anger. They spend a great deal of energy resisting stressful situations, extending their duration and intensity. They complain, fret, argue, and have difficulty identifying options for alleviating or managing their stress, and therefore feel trapped by their circumstances.

Positive people, on the other hand, are more readily able to recognize the stress they feel as an elective condition. They more readily see stress as a choice and actively take action to alleviate and/or counteract it. For instance, a positive person under stress can choose to channel that stress into productive expenditures of energy like exercising or tackling personal projects. Positive people are also more likely to view stressful situations as part of a larger picture or purpose (i.e., the stress of a final exam being off-set by the knowledge that it is another step in earning a desired degree). **THEY ARE MORE LIKELY TO SEE CHALLENGES AS OPPORTUNITIES, NOT THREATS.**

Most importantly, positive people are more actively aware that much of our stress is self-inflicted, and that stress is an "elective" condition. Stress is a choice. We all have the right to determine the priorities in our lives – what is or is not important. However, when in a negative mindset, we find it difficult to see the big picture and make conscious decisions about what really matters and what doesn't. In its essence, stress comes from the feeling we **HAVE** to do something versus **WANTING** to do something.

STRESS IN RELATIONSHIPS

All of us need to work on our relationship with stress – and isn't that where most of our stress comes from – our relationships. Healthy, vibrant relationships can be a source of great joy. However, many times our relationships can generate great stress. Whether it is with a spouse/significant other, child, parent, sibling, friend, boss, co-worker, neighbor, or other interpersonal relationship, these relationships are often major contributors to the stress we experience.

ACCORDING TO A 2003 REVIEW IN THE *JOURNAL OF PHYSIOLOGY AND BEHAVIOR*, DISTRESSED MARRIAGES ARE A MAJOR SOURCE OF STRESS FOR COUPLES. In fact, the study found that unhappily married people generally are worse off in their well-being than unmarried people. Marital stress can spill over into the workplace, too.

ACCORDING TO A 2005 ARTICLE IN THE *ANNALS OF BEHAVIORAL MEDICINE*, DOMESTIC STRAIN CAN INFLUENCE HOW WELL PEOPLE FUNCTION OVER THE WORKDAY, AWAY FROM HOME. The researchers measured the blood pressure and levels of the stress hormone cortisol of 105 middle-age men and women, and compared them to the self-reported stress levels. They found that those with more marital concerns reported greater stress throughout the day, had higher blood pressure in the middle of the workday and higher morning cortisol levels. These factors can, over time, combine to increase the risk of obesity, diabetes, depression, heart attack and stroke, the study concluded. In addition, our intrapersonal relationships with things like our relationship with our jobs, with money, with our health, and, most importantly, with ourselves, cause considerable stress in our lives.

In the next RX+ Script, we will continue to look at stress as it applies to relationships both with others, but especially with your **SELF**.

℞+ SCRIPT 3

Focus on Positive Relationships

Build and maintain positive relationships in your life with others, and especially yourself.

THE BELIEF:

I PLACE A PRIORITY ON MY RELATIONSHIP WITH MYSELF. I HAVE STRONG POSITIVE RELATIONSHIPS WITH OTHERS.

If you are reading this book, then you are taking an active interest in your health. **BUT, DO YOU REALIZE THAT THE QUALITY OF YOUR RELATIONSHIPS CAN BE JUST AS TOXIC TO YOUR HEALTH AS FAST FOOD OR A TOXIC ENVIRONMENT.** In fact, unhealthy relationships can turn into exactly that – a toxic internal environment that can lead to stress, depression, anxiety, and major medical problems. Our social connections aren't just about enjoyment and camaraderie, they also influence our long-term health in ways every bit as powerful as adequate sleep, a good diet, and not smoking. Dozens of studies have shown that people who have satisfying relationships with family, friends, and their community are happier, have fewer health problems, and live longer.

Conversely, a relative lack of social ties is associated with depression and later-life cognitive decline, as well as with increased mortality. **ONE STUDY, WHICH EXAMINED DATA FROM MORE THAN 309,000 PEOPLE, FOUND THAT LACK OF STRONG RELATIONSHIPS INCREASED THE RISK OF PREMATURE DEATH FROM ALL CAUSES BY 50%** — an effect on mortality risk roughly **COMPARABLE TO SMOKING UP TO FIFTEEN CIGARETTES A DAY, AND GREATER THAN OBESITY OR PHYSICAL INACTIVITY.** Simply put, the relationships that you develop and maintain in your life determine how long you will live. So, rather than worrying about the latest health trend, obsessing over what you are eating or protecting yourself from various safety hazards, **IF YOU REALLY WANT TO TAKE CONTROL OVER YOUR HEALTH AND WELLNESS, TAKE A GOOD HARD LOOK AT YOUR RELATIONSHIPS.**

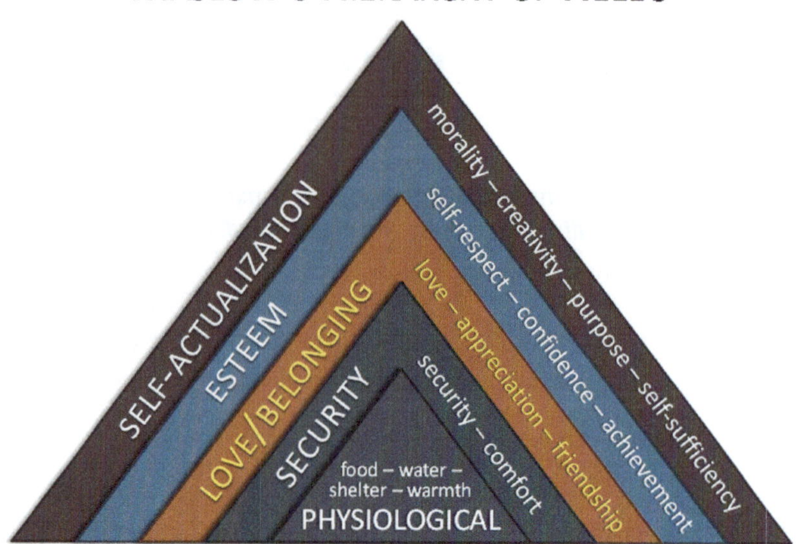

Maslow's Hierarchy of Needs

For humans, social interaction is a basic human need. Psychologist Abraham Maslow first introduced his concept of a hierarchy of needs in his 1943 paper "A Theory of Human Motivation" and his subsequent book, **Motivation and Personality**. This hierarchy suggests that people are motivated to fulfill basic needs before moving on to other, more advanced needs.

This hierarchy is most often displayed as a pyramid. The lowest levels of the pyramid are made up of the most basic needs, while the more complex needs are located at the top of the pyramid. Needs at the bottom of the pyramid are basic physical requirements including the need for food, water, sleep, and warmth. Once these lower-level needs have been met, people can move on to the next level of needs, which are for safety and security.

As people progress up the pyramid, needs become increasingly psychological and social. Soon, the need for love, friendship, and intimacy become important. Having relationships with others is a primal need that we all have as humans. We are social creatures and need the companionship and sense of belonging that comes from social interactions to feel fulfilled in our lives. Our relationships define our lives in many ways, and they have a very real impact on our health.

Relationships and Longevity

Researchers at Brigham Young University and the University of North Carolina at Chapel Hill pooled data from 148 studies on health outcomes and social relationships — every research paper on the topic they could find, involving more than 300,000 men and women across the developed world — and **FOUND THAT THOSE WITH POOR SOCIAL CONNECTIONS HAD ON AVERAGE 50% HIGHER ODDS OF DEATH IN THE STUDY'S FOLLOW-UP PERIOD (AN AVERAGE OF 7.5 YEARS) THAN PEOPLE WITH MORE ROBUST SOCIAL TIES.**

That boost in longevity is about as large as the mortality difference observed between smokers and nonsmokers, the study's authors say. In fact, the risk of death associated with having poor social connections is more than the risk of many other well-known lifestyle factors, including lack of exercise and obesity.

"This is not just a few studies here and there," says Julianne Holt-Lunstad, associate professor of psychology at Brigham Young University and lead author of "Social Relationships and Mortality Risk: A Meta-analytic Review" published in 2010 in *PLoS Medicine*. "I'm hoping there will be recognition from the medical community, the public-health community and even the general public about the importance of this."

Relationships and Stress

Our family and friends support us in a number of ways: emotionally, spiritually, even physically if we are injured and incapable of functioning on our own. But, the influence of social ties may be even more powerful than that. Social relationships, it seems, also help our bodies help themselves.

Recent studies have shown that, in stressful situations, blood pressure and heart rate will increase less when people are accompanied by a person who is close to them. Brain imaging also shows neurological differences between a person who is alone and a person who has support. In a laboratory-induced stress situation, the brain activity in the anterior cingulate cortex (a region activated in times of stress) was less stimulated when the subject had a close friend or relative alongside them during the test.

This phenomenon is not limited to adult stress. In an experiment published recently, children who were allowed to talk to their mothers after a stressful encounter — giving an impromptu speech or doing math problems in public — showed increased levels of oxytocin, a neurotransmitter thought to dampen the hormonal stress response, compared with children who did not have contact with their mothers.

> ***A healthy social life may be as good for your long-term health as avoiding cigarettes.***
>
> Julianne Hold-Lunstad
> Professor of Psychology at Brigham Young University

Relationships and Health

In one of the most famous experiments on health and social life, Sheldon Cohen, a professor of psychology at Carnegie Mellon University, exposed hundreds of healthy volunteers to the common cold virus, then quarantined them for several days. Cohen showed that the study participants with more social connections and with more diverse social networks — that is, with friends from a variety of social contexts, such as work, sports teams and church — were less likely to develop a cold than the more socially isolated study participants.

The immune systems of people with lots of friends simply worked better, fighting off the cold virus often without symptoms. Studies suggest that the immune response may be affected by stress hormones — catecholamines and glucocorticoids — so that a strong social life can positively affect immune function by helping people keep physiological stress in check.

> A large Swedish study of people ages 75 and over concluded that dementia risk was lowest in those with a variety of satisfying contacts with friends and relatives.

Positive Versus Negative Relationships

Not all relationships are created equal. Positive relationships provide positive health results. Negative relationships are actually harmful to us.

According to a 2000 study published in the *Journal of the American Medical Association*, **WOMEN WHO REPORTED MODERATE TO SEVERE MARITAL STRAIN WERE 2.9 TIMES MORE LIKELY TO NEED HEART SURGERY, SUFFER HEART ATTACKS OR DIE OF HEART DISEASE THAN WOMEN WITHOUT MARITAL STRESS.** This finding held even when researchers adjusted for other factors such as age, smoking habits, diabetes, blood pressure and "bad" cholesterol levels.

These results were echoed by another study published in the *American Journal of Cardiology* in 2006, which showed that marital quality and social support are especially important in the development and management of chronic diseases such as congestive heart failure. The study found that patients with the most severe heart disease and poorest marriages had the highest risk of dying over a four-year period. The four-year survival rate of those with severe heart disease and poor marriages was 42%, compared with 78% among patients with milder heart disease and good marriages.

According to Howard Rankin, a clinical psychologist and founder of The Rankin Center for Neuroscience and Integrative Health, a bad marriage or relationship can be as hard on you as any other damaging health choice. "The impact of a negative relationship goes beyond self-esteem, into the very body itself," Dr. Rankin explains. "**UNDER CHRONIC STRESS, THE IMMUNE SYSTEM BREAKS DOWN, LEADING TO A WHOLE HOST OF DISEASES.**

A recent study of breast cancer patients showed that many women believed that their cancer was caused by stress. Technically, no one gets cancer because of stress. What does happen is that the suppression of the immune system by prolonged stress makes it more likely that the body can't fight off the cancer and creates an environment where cancer cells can grow."

Mirror Neurons

Imagine you are walking through a park when, out of nowhere, a man in front of you gets smacked in the head by an errant Frisbee. Automatically, you cringe in sympathy. Or, think back to when you have watched a basketball or football game and remember how you felt your own heart race with excitement as your team made a critical basket or touchdown.

For years, such experiences have puzzled psychologists, neuroscientists and philosophers, who have wondered why we react at such a gut level to other people's actions. How do we understand, so immediately and instinctively, the thoughts, feelings and intentions of other people?

About two decades ago, a team of Italian researchers stumbled on an answer. While observing monkeys' brains, they noticed that certain cells activated both when a monkey performed an action and when that monkey watched another monkey perform the same action. If you will forgive the pun, it really was a case of "monkey see, monkey do."

Mirror neurons, as they have been dubbed, are the scientific adjunct to what people have known for millennia; humans are naturally empathic. When we see someone else feeling or doing something, we can tune in and feel it ourselves. Ask any entertainer and they will tell you that causing their audience to feel something is their ultimate goal. Our empathic abilities are highly tuned and the neural mechanism behind them is both involuntary and automatic. We don't have to think about what other people are doing or feeling, we often simply know and act accordingly.

> ***It seems we're wired to see other people as similar to us, rather than different. At the root, as humans we identify the person we're facing as someone like ourselves.***
>
> Neuroscientist Vittorio Gallese, M.D., Ph.D.
> University of Parma, Italy

So, why are our mirror neurons and empathic abilities important? Because, we can leverage them to our benefit... or our detriment. Think about it. **IF YOU ARE SURROUNDING YOURSELF WITH PEOPLE WHO TEND TO THINK AND/OR ACT NEGATIVELY, THEN YOUR MIRROR NEURONS WILL CAUSE YOU TO FEEL AND ACT NEGATIVELY, AS WELL.** Your tendency will be to automatically tune into the negativity around you. Conversely, if you surround yourself with people who think and act positively, you will automatically begin to absorb and reflect their positivity.

Evidence of this begins early in life. Visit any middle or high school and you'll notice that children who spend time together often dress and act similarly (i.e., why many parents worry when their children begin to hang out with a bad crowd). This tendency persists throughout our life into old age. Some controversial studies have shown that people who elect to live in retirement communities often age faster than those who live in their own homes. This is especially true if relatively healthy and active seniors move into a community with an older, more infirm population. Older persons who a few weeks before were walking erect will become more stooped, as their mirror neurons tell their brain to mimic what they see around them. Conversely, studies have also shown that elderly persons who are surrounded by younger more active people actually can increase their cognitive and physical performance, as their brain tells them to mirror the behavior of what they see around them.

JUST AS YOU ARE WHAT YOU EAT, YOU THINK AND BEHAVE LIKE THOSE YOU CHOOSE TO SPEND TIME WITH. When it comes to being and staying positive, the company you keep and the relationships you foster are key. But, first and foremost, the most important relationship you have is with you. **BEFORE YOU CAN BEGIN TO HAVE POSITIVE RELATIONSHIPS WITH OTHERS, YOU FIRST MUST BUILD A STRONG, POSITIVE RELATIONSHIP WITH YOURSELF.**

POSITIVE RELATIONSHIP WITH SELF

Within each one of us are two personalities: a positive one and a negative one. Our positive personality believes that there is good in the world, that people are inherently well intentioned, and that life is a gift. Our negative side sees the world as a bad place, filled with dangers and pitfalls. Our negative side is distrustful, judgmental and fearful. This internal duality works like preset stations on a radio. We can either set our internal and external sensors to receive positive signals, or we can set them to receive negative signals. It is all in how we choose to tune in.

SADLY, FOR MANY IN OUR WORLD, NEGATIVITY TENDS TO BE THE DEFAULT STATION. When you ask people how they are doing, you usually hear what is wrong with their lives. If you ask someone about love, they will most likely talk about heartbreak. If you ask them about their health, they will tell you about their illness(es).

But, what station you tune into – positive or negative – is a choice. There is an old story of a Native American Elder who is speaking to a group of children. He tells them, "There is a white wolf and a black wolf that lives in each of our hearts. The black wolf is filled with fear, anger, envy, jealousy, greed, and arrogance. The white wolf is filled with peace, love, hope, courage, humility, compassion, and faith. The two wolves battle constantly." One of the children asks, "Grandfather, which of the two wolves wins?" The elder replies, "The one we feed."

FOCUSING ON THE POSITIVE DOESN'T MEAN THAT YOU KEEP YOUR HEAD IN THE SAND AND IGNORE LIFE'S LESS PLEASANT SITUATIONS. Positive thinking just means that you approach the unpleasantness in a more positive and productive way. You think the best is going to happen, not the worst. How do you do this? The key is to start tuning into your own self-talk.

The Voice in Your Head

Self-talk is the endless stream of unspoken thoughts that run through our heads every day. Self-talk includes our conscious thoughts, as well as our unconscious assumptions and beliefs. Much of our self-talk can be reasonable:

- "I am good at my job."
- "I know I am going to have a great workout later."
- "I am going to ace my exam."

However, our self-talk can also be negative and self-defeating:

- "I know I'm going to fail."
- "I am unattractive and will never find the right relationship."
- "I can't do that."
- "I am hopeless."

As we start to become aware of our inner self-talk, many people are surprised by how negative it can be. In fact, people often think far worse of themselves than they ever do of others.

However, the more aware of your self-talk you become, the more you will be able to choose your thoughts and rewire the beliefs behind them.

Emotional Self-Check

The best way to check your self-talk is by tuning into your emotions. Take a moment and think of something challenging you have to accomplish in the next few weeks. It might be a presentation you have to make in front of a group, a difficult project you have to complete for work, or a critical conversation you have to have with a loved one. You'll know you have hit on the right thing when you start to feel the stress of fear, anxiety, nervousness, and/or anger.

These negative emotions are clear indications that your self-talk regarding this event or situation may not be positive. When you feel anxious, depressed or stressed-out, your self-talk is likely to become extreme, and you'll be more likely to expect the worst and focus on the most negative aspects of your situation.

The next step is to test and challenge yourself about what thoughts are going through your mind about this. You do this by asking questions.

- Do I really believe what I am thinking is true?
- Am I jumping to negative conclusions?
- Are there any other ways that I could look at this situation?
- If I were being positive, how would I perceive this situation?
- Is this situation as bad as I am making it out to be? Could I be exaggerating things in any way?
- What is the worst thing that could happen? How likely is it?
- Is there anything good about this situation?
- Is there something I can learn from this situation, to help me do it better next time?
- Will this matter in a few days/weeks/years?
- Is thinking this way helping me to feel good or to achieve my goals?
- What beliefs do I hold that are behind these negative thoughts?
- What beliefs do I hold that could change this situation from a negative one to a positive one?

Recognizing that your current way of thinking might be **SELF-DEFEATING** (e.g., it doesn't make you feel good or help you to get what you want) can sometimes motivate you to look at things from a different perspective. You can conquer your negative self-talk today by challenging yourself with these questions every time you catch yourself thinking something negative to or about yourself.

How to Rewire and Think Positive Thoughts

Because the mind is a magnet, consciously focusing on the good things in life will bring them to you. Think about the negative and that is what you will attract. One popular method to help you reprogram your thoughts and beliefs is through **OPTIMISTIC AUTOSUGGESTION (I.E., POSITIVE AFFIRMATIONS THAT TRIGGER A POSITIVE MINDSET)**. French psychologist, Émile Coué (1857-1926) introduced optimistic autosuggestion as a method of psychotherapy, healing, and self-improvement.

Growth Mindset

In her book, ***Mindset****, Stanford University psychologist Carol Dweck outlines two distinctly different mindsets about how people view their potential and talent:*

1. **Fixed mindset:** *the belief that talent is fixed (i.e., that we are born with a certain level of ability and that innate talent dictates our success)*
2. **Growth/incremental mindset:** *the belief that talent is nurtured and is malleable (i.e., people can develop and grow their skills).*

While Dweck does not conclusively address the "nature versus nurture" debate as to whether talent/potential is 100% innate or 100% developed, she does make a case that our abilities are very much affected by our beliefs as to whether or not we can improve. In her studies of both children and adults, she found that those who believe that their skills levels can improve stood a much better chance of actually improve their skills.

For example, Dweck and some colleagues told junior high students that the brain is like a muscle that can be developed and strengthened through practice. This simple but elegant explanation led these students to higher levels of motivation and better grades! The students' belief that they could improve allowed them to improve.

Coué's infamous and often replicated auto-suggestion was:

"EVERY DAY, IN EVERY WAY, I AM GETTING BETTER AND BETTER."

He instructed his patients to repeat this magical mantra every day especially at the beginning and end of each day. This simple phrase produced remarkable health enhancements for Coué's patients during his time, and continues to work for many people today.

The basic theory behind optimistic auto-suggestion is that by consciously repeating positive statements, people begin to change their way of thinking (rewiring their brain) and manifest the positive in their bodies and lives. They simply rewire themselves to think and believe more positively.

How can you start focusing on the positive more actively? It is not as easy as one might "believe." Think back to the story at the beginning of Chapter

9. Did you think you were more likely to get the bullets or the bucks? Start thinking less about the bullets and more about the bucks and see what happens. **BEGIN AND END EACH DAY POSITIVELY** by mentally or verbally repeating a positive affirmation. You can borrow Émile Coué's "Every day in every way, I am getting better and better." Better yet, make up your own optimistic autosuggestion that will help you "rewire" yourself toward the positive.

Physician and psychiatrist Dr. Daniel G. Amen suggests combatting your **ANTS (AUTOMATIC NEGATIVE THOUGHTS)** with conscious positive thoughts. His research has shown that positive thoughts and affirmations in our conscious mind can have a profound effect on our cells, our behaviors, our health and our longevity. When you consciously focus on positive thoughts, chemicals are released in the brain that translate into good feelings in the body.

Remember, when it comes to your health and wellness, you come first. It is only when you have a strong positive relationship with your **SELF** – your beliefs about your basic nature and the nature of the world – that you can build rewarding, positive relationships with others.

> ***"What goes on in your mind all day long can determine whether your behavior is self-defeating or self-promoting."***
>
> Daniel G. Amen, M.D
> Physician, Psychiatrist and Author

RELATIONSHIPS WITH OTHERS

Most of us can identify our most positive relationships. They are the ones that make us feel good. When we interact and engage with the people in these relationships, we feel joyful, comfortable, energized and uplifted. Even when we have challenging moments with these individuals, there is an underlying sense of closeness, a willingness to move past any issues because of how much we cherish their presence in our lives.

Our negative relationships, on the other hand, are sometimes more difficult to identify because of the beliefs we hold about them. It is difficult to say that a relationship with a sibling, child, spouse, or long-time friend is negative because of the strong ties, history and expectations we have about these types of relationships.

Remember, it is much easier to stay positive if you are in like company of other positive, upbeat people. Positive people rub off on each other.

However, it is important to look at all the main relationships in your life and reevaluate which work for you and which do not. If a decades-long friendship is no longer supportive and mutually beneficial, you may need to consider cutting the ties. If a boyfriend or girlfriend is treating you poorly, you need to consider confronting them about the issues and/or possibly moving on to another more positive relationship. We all need to recognize that detachment can be difficult, given the realities of a situation, but is sometimes necessary.

One of the best ways to reduce your stress and give yourself a boost of happiness—and health— is to remember that you have the right to choose the relationships that serve your highest good.

Identifying Negative Relationships

There are many types of negative relationships, including relationships of convenience, relationships of advantage, relationships of attachment, relationships filled with fantasies and expectations that will fail in the face of a real life situation, etc. Again, the key indicator that a relationship is no longer working for you are your emotions. If you are consistently feeling badly when you interact and engage with someone, then it is time to ask yourself some serious questions about the relationship.

1. When you are with [the person], do you usually feel content, even energized? Or do you often feel unfulfilled and drained?
2. After you spend time with him/her, do you usually feel better or worse about yourself?

Fighting dirty, cold wars, the silent treatment, stomping off, slamming doors, never reaching a resolution ... did you know that all these behaviors have a negative effect not only on the health of your relationship but also on your physical health? The stress of being in a bad relationship can affect your physical health now and for years to come.

---

3. Do you feel physically and/or emotionally safe with this person, or do you feel threatened or in danger?
4. Is there a fairly equal "give and take" in the relationship? Or do you feel like you're always giving and he/she is always taking?
5. Is the relationship characterized by feelings of security and contentment, or drama and angst?
6. Do you feel like he/she is happy with who you are? Or do you feel like you have to change to make him/her happy?

Now compare your answers to the following characteristics of healthy versus toxic relationships.

Healthy Relationships	Toxic Relationships
• Compassionate	• Insecurity
• Secure	• Abuse of power and control
• Safe	• Demanding
• Sharing	• Selfish
• Listening	• Self-centeredness
• Mutual love/caring	• Criticism
• Healthy debate/disagreements	• Negativity
• Respectfulness even during differences in opinion	• Dishonesty and distrust
	• Demeaning comments/attitudes
	• Jealousy

Changing Toxic Relationships

The first step to changing a toxic relationship is to recognize you are in one. Many people in unhealthy relationships are in denial, even when friends or family members are seeing the danger signs and make mention of their concerns.

The next step, equally as important, is to believe that you deserve to be treated with respect, love, and compassion. There are many reasons why people stay in unhealthy relationships, but one common reason is underlying low self-esteem that makes some people believe that they do not deserve anything better. This kind of change in thinking, however, may not come easily and may require professional support from an objective third party, such as a counselor or a life coach.

Once you come to believe that you deserve to be treated differently, the next step is likely to come easier -- addressing the negative behavior when it occurs. When doing this, use "I" statements as much as possible to reduce the likelihood of a defensive reaction. For example, you may want to say something like, "I feel like you find fault in almost everything I do and it makes me feel [fill in the blank]. I (love, respect, care about, etc.) you, and I'd appreciate it if you would stop [fill in the blank]."

> ***With all humility and gentleness, with patience, showing forbearance to one another in love, being diligent to preserve the unity of the Spirit in the bond of peace.***
>
> Ephesians 4:2-3

Finally, if nothing you do or say changes the negative behavior, you should consider separating yourself or at least distancing yourself from the source of the toxicity. For partners, this may mean separation (temporary or permanent). For parents and children, this may mean having less contact. For coworkers, this may mean distancing yourself as much as possible. The most important thing is to take action. Doing nothing will only expose you to the unhealthy physical and psychological effects of stress and ongoing conflict.

POSITIVE RELATIONSHIPS ARE AN IMPORTANT PART OF THE FORMULA FOR A HEALTHY, WELL-BALANCED LIFE. As you plan for your health and longevity, do not leave out this important ingredient.

CONDUCT YOUR OWN RELATIONAL AUDIT

The following Relational ® Audit can help you identify the key relationships you have in your life and their level of priority in terms of actively promoting positive relational well-being.

Most people have relationships that they would like to develop more fully with key family members or friends, potential mentors, etc. It is important for us to periodically step back and assess our "big picture" relational network to see if we are fostering the right relationships in the most positive ways.

Current Relationships

At times, we do not give enough time and attention to the relationships in our lives. These can be personal relationships, professional relationships, or even our relationship with our self and/or a higher power. Take a moment to review your currently relationships to see if there are any that you could enhance.

1. Are there any relationships at home, work, or elsewhere that you want to engage in more fully? ☐ Yes ☐ No
   If yes, list them by name or group (i.e., family members, friends, coworkers, peers, etc.):

New Relationships

It is also helpful to occasionally step back and see if we need to develop relationships with people currently outside of our relational network. This is especially true during times of transitions or change (like a move to a new work situation or geographic relocation).

2. Are there any relationships that you want to initiate? ☐ Yes ☐ No

   If yes, list them by name or group (i.e., new neighbor, spiritual advisor, life coach, mentor, etc.):

Relationships That Need To End/Shift

On occasion, we all need to assess whether we need to end certain relationships we are currently engaged in (with a spouse, family member or long-time friend). Remember, that it is natural for relationships to evolve over time. Our interests change and our priorities shift, sometimes to the extent that they are no longer consistent with others in our lives. When we are children, we are more readily open to the natural flow of people in and out of our lives (teachers, friends, etc.). Most children are very open to playing with new people and do not attach to the idea that they may or may not ever see them again. It is important to remember that a change in a relationship does not necessarily mean that you will never have that level of closeness with someone again. This negative belief often keeps us locked in existing relationships rather than allowing us to explore more positive and beneficial potential relationships.

3. Are there any relationships that you should terminate/shift? ☐ Yes ☐ No

   If yes, list them by name or group (i.e., spouse/lover, family member, friend, etc.):

℞⁺ SCRIPT 4

Cultivate Happiness

Actively seek happiness in your life. Recognize that happiness is a choice dependent not on circumstances, but on belief.

THE BELIEF:

I CHOOSE TO BE HAPPY TODAY AND EVERY DAY.

A positive mindset is grounded in a foundation of happiness. The pursuit of happiness is behind everything we do. From the moment we get up in the morning to the moment we go to bed, all of our actions and behaviors are an effort to seek happiness in some form. It is why we pray, get married, go to college, slave through tiresome days at the office, endure heartache, buy into fads, and move through what some days can be the grind of everyday life. We are seeking that ever evasive and elusive condition that will bring about happiness.

Happiness is why we work so hard to find:

- The perfect relationship
- The right job
- The best health
- The perfect dream house/car
- And so much more...

We dedicate an enormous amount of time, energy and effort just to find some measure of happiness. Yet, so often, we go to bed at the end of the day with our happiness quota unfulfilled. We feel disappointment, frustration, confusion, and even physical pain from the lack of happiness in our lives. **WE CANNOT UNDERSTAND THAT AFTER TRYING SO HARD AND WORKING SO DILIGENTLY THAT WE ARE SIMPLY NOT HAPPY. OR IS IT THAT WE JUST "THINK" WE ARE UNHAPPY?**

> "Happiness is the meaning and the purpose of life, the whole aim and end of human existence."
>
> — Aristotle

Before we look into how we can cultivate happiness in our lives, let's first take a quick look at how happiness works in the brain.

The Physiology of Happiness

In her book, **Mind Over Medicine**, Dr. Lissa Rankin describes how through magnetic resonance imaging (MRIs) and electroencephalograms (EEGs), scientists are studying where happiness happens in the brain. **Consensus is now pointing to the left prefrontal cortex as the "hub of happiness" in the brain, but the sub-cortex at the bottom of the brain is also involved.** When research subjects report that they feel good or happy, these two areas of the brain "light up" with a burst of electrical activity and blood flow, proving that happiness is not just a feeling, but an actual physical state of the brain.

Richard Davidson, a professor of psychology and psychiatry, and associate scientist Antoine Lutz, both at the University of Wisconsin-Madison, studied a group of Buddhist monks entering a "bliss" state during meditation. The 16 monks included in the study had practiced meditation for a minimum of 10,000 hours. They were compared to 16 age-matched control subjects with no previous training who were taught the fundamentals of meditation two weeks before the brain scanning took place. **When observed via an MRI, as the monks moved deeper into a trance-like state, the prefrontal lobe of their brains crackled with increased electrical signals at a tremendous rate.** While the control subjects also showed some activity in that area of the brain, it was minor in comparison to that of monks who practiced meditation on a far more regular basis.

The findings supported Davidson and Lutz's working assumption that through training, people can develop skills that promote happiness and compassion. **"People are not just stuck at their respective set points,"** says Davidson. **"We can take advantage of our brain's plasticity and train it to enhance these qualities."**

The Happy Versus Unhappy Brain

What is the physical difference between a "happy brain" and one that isn't happy? It has something to do with neurotransmitters, the chemicals that carry the signals from one brain cell (called neuron) to another. **A "HAPPINESS" REACTION IN THE BRAIN IS ACTIVATED WITH THE HELP OF NEUROTRANSMITTERS LIKE DOPAMINE, OXYTOCIN, ENDORPHINS, NITRIC ACID, AND SEROTONIN.** Each of these neurotransmitters is triggered by particular types of happiness.

For example, **ONE WAY TO TRIGGER HAPPINESS IS THE ANTICIPATION RESPONSE TO A POSITIVE FUTURE EXPERIENCE (I.E., THAT FEELING YOU GET WHEN YOU ARE LOOKING FORWARD TO SOMETHING).** It can be something as simple as looking forward to having dinner with a friend, or anticipating the release of the next book in a series you enjoy. It can be as profound as anticipating seeing your newborn child for the first time or being reunited with a loved one after a long period of separation. These feelings of happy anticipation are connected to the release of dopamine in your body. Dopamine is the body's chemical translator of happiness, and promotes a feeling of increased energy and, with the help of endorphins, is a natural pain suppressant.

Other neurotransmitters are triggered by other aspects of happiness. Oxytocin has earned the nickname "the cuddle hormone," and is released when you feel love or sensations of physical pleasure. Made in the hypothalamus and secreted by the pituitary gland, oxytocin reduces inflammation and stimulates the release of endorphins, which are known as the body's natural morphine. **ENDORPHINS REDUCE PAIN AND LEAD TO EUPHORIC FEELINGS (LIKE THE "RUNNER'S HIGH").**

By having a greater understanding how happiness works in the brain, more effective strategies can be created for treating clinical depression and other mood disorders. The findings from happiness studies and depression research can be useful in decreasing depression as well as increasing happiness. **IN TURN, GREATER HAPPINESS AND LIFE SATISFACTION CAN HELP PEOPLE BECOME HEALTHIER AND LIVE LONGER.**

Learned Helplessness Versus Learned Happiness

A recent study separated tumor-laden rats into two groups. One group was repeatedly subjected to shocks that they could not escape or avoid. The other group was given an outlet to avoid the shocks.

The first group that could not avoid the shocks acquired a condition of **LEARNED HELPLESSNESS.** They had been conditioned that they could not escape their fate of being repeatedly shocked, and their depression and unhappiness made them far more susceptible to cancer, infection and other immune-related conditions. The rats that could avoid the shocks, however, were healthier and lived considerably longer.

Sadly, rats are not the only ones who can be conditioned into feelings of learned helplessness and unhappiness. All of us can fall prey to the sense that happiness is an unattainable and ephemeral goal. However, we can also condition ourselves right back out of that belief. All we have to do is deepen our understanding of what happiness really is.

The Key to Happiness

THE KEY TO HAPPINESS IS RECOGNIZING THAT IT IS A CHOICE! We choose to be happy... or not. It comes down to perception and the mind. We foster a belief that we are happy – or – we choose to be unhappy. As our brain accepts this belief, so does health and wellness follow. Consider the short parable below, which shows how even in difficult times we still can choose to be happy.

The 92-year-old, petite, well-poised and proud lady, who is fully dressed each morning by 8 o'clock, with her hair fashionably coifed and makeup perfectly applied, even though she is legally blind, moved to a nursing home today. Her husband of 70 years recently passed away, making the move necessary. After many hours of waiting patiently in the lobby of the nursing home, she smiled sweetly when told her room was ready.

As she maneuvered her walker to the elevator, I provided a visual description of her tiny room, including the eyelet sheets that had been hung on her window. "I love it," she stated with the enthusiasm of an 8-year-old having just been presented with a new puppy.

"Mrs. Jones, you haven't seen the room .... just wait."

"That doesn't have anything to do with it," she replied. "Happiness is something you decide on

ahead of time. Whether I like my room or not doesn't depend on how the furniture is arranged ... it's how I arrange my mind. I already decided to love it.... It's a decision I make every morning when I wake up. I have a choice; I can spend the day in bed recounting the difficulty I have with the parts of my body that no longer work, or get out of bed and be thankful for the ones that do. Each day is a gift, and as long as my eyes open I'll focus on the new day and all the happy memories I've stored away ... just for this time in my life."

Author Unknown

THE FIRST STEP TO CULTIVATING HAPPINESS IS TO ACCEPT BOTH THE POWER AND RESPONSIBILITY YOU HAVE TO CHOOSE HAPPINESS IN EVERY MOMENT AND EVERY DAY. No matter what the situation or circumstance, you accept that you can choose to be happy. You do this by working to change how you look at happiness. It is all about your perspective.

DEFINING HAPPINESS

What does happiness mean to you? There are several common misconceptions about what happiness can be in our lives. Below are just a few examples.

- *HAPPINESS IS PLEASURE:* Not necessarily. Pleasure is often just a sensation of instant gratification – physical or mental. Think about taking a bite of your favorite dessert. It might be a pleasurable experience, but once the dessert is gone, your pleasure is over. **HAPPINESS IS SOMETHING MUCH MORE PROFOUND THAT EXISTS BEYOND THE CONDITION OF A PARTICULAR SITUATION OR CIRCUMSTANCE.**
- *HAPPINESS IS COMFORT OR SECURITY:* We live most of our lives with threats to our safety and security – our jobs, our children out at night, our health, etc. The truth is that security or lack of it is based on perception. **HAPPINESS IS CHOOSING TO LIVE WELL IN THE MIDST OF INSTABILITY AND UNCERTAINTY.**
- *I DON'T DESERVE HAPPINESS:* Says who? This is one of the biggest self-limiting beliefs. Happiness is for everyone, no matter where you come from or what you have done. **HAPPINESS IS OPEN-SOURCE, AND ALL YOU HAVE TO DO IS TAP INTO IT.**

- *IT'S IMPOSSIBLE TO FIND HAPPINESS IN THIS WORLD:* This is another example of a self-limiting belief. Despite what the news media would have you believe, there is more good in the world than you might think. **IF YOU LOOK FOR IT, HAPPINESS IS ACTUALLY EASIER TO FIND THAN UNHAPPINESS.**

These are but some of the many misconceptions about happiness. You would do well to take some time to write your own definition of happiness and discover what it is you are really seeking from your life.

HAPPINESS FROM WITHIN

For most of us, happiness is a pursuit that occurs outside of ourselves. We are constantly asking ourselves what it is that we can add or change that will take our lives from difficult, challenging, unsatisfied or simply okay to vibrantly, ridiculously happy.

Consider the equation below. It is actually a belief that most of us hold. All that we are and have today isn't enough. We just need to add ________ [fill in the blank] to be happy. This belief is constantly reinforced by the media and our consumption-driven culture and lifestyle. We are pushed to seek happiness external to ourselves. We aren't enough. Our happiness is dependent on something else, usually something that is available for purchase or acquisition.

Whether it is a new relationship through an online dating site, the latest and most technologically advanced smartphone, a trendy new outfit, or an

unbeatable leak-proof diaper, we are told again and again that there is something missing in our lives. Once we have it, we will be happy. If you doubt it, just look at the faces of the people in the advertisements and you will see how happy you can be if only you add [fill in the blank] to your life.

But, even if we are able to get all of the [fill in the blanks] we want, many of us remain unhappy. The hard-earned degree, the engagement ring, the new promotion, the vacation of our dreams... all provide only short-term joy unless we embrace that happiness doesn't come from outside of us. **IT COMES FROM DEEP WITHIN, AND THE KNOWLEDGE OF WHAT IT IS WE REALLY, REALLY WANT FROM OUR LIVES.**

WHAT DO YOU REALLY, REALLY WANT?

At first glance, knowing what we really, really want may seem an easy question to answer. But, if we take the time to focus on it, it is actually a difficult question for most of us to answer.

There are usually several levels of answers to this question. At first we might answer with something like:

- I want a new job.
- I want a new relationship.
- I want a new house.

But, these are only superficial responses. The answer to what we really, really want lies behind them. What is it about a new job that appeals to you? Why would a new relationship make your life better? What can a new house offer you that you don't have in your current living situation?

Often the answers to what "we really, really want" run much deeper:

- I want to feel safe and secure.
- I want to be regarded well by my family and friends.
- I want to be recognized for my hard work.
- I want to have the financial freedom not to feel stress about money.

As you begin to dig deep inside of yourself, your wants become more elemental and rooted in what you really seek out of life. **KNOWING "WHAT YOU REALLY, REALLY WANT" ALLOWS YOU TO REFOCUS YOUR EFFORTS TOWARD THOSE THINGS THAT WILL TRULY BRING YOU HAPPINESS, FROM THE INSIDE OUT.**

Happiness is Now!

Just the other day, an employee at my local hardware store told me to "Have a good day!" as I was leaving the store. I replied in kind, wishing him a good day, as well. At this point, it was a typical polite exchange that occurs countless times a day almost everywhere you go. Except, in this case, the store employee went on to say, "Oh, I always have a good day. I gave up bad days years ago, and I am much better for it!"

So often, we push our happiness off into the future:

- "Once I finish my degree, I will be happy."
- "Once I retire, I will be happy."
- "Once I lose 10 pounds, I will be happy."

Or, if we are not projecting into the future, we will reminisce about the past.

- The happiest time in my life was when I was in college.
- The happiest moment in my life was when my first child was born.
- I have never been happier than when I travelled through Europe right after high school.

The question you need to be asking is while you are projecting into the future and/or reminiscing about the past, **WHAT ARE YOU SACRIFICING IN THE PRESENT?** Now is all you really have. The past is gone and the future is not here... but you are! The only way you can ensure your happiness is by finding it in the preset moment.

The Science Behind "Be Here Now!"

People talk about "Be Here Now," an adage that speaks volumes of importance, but offers very little instruction on how to do it. But, science is starting to add its weight behind the "Be Here Now" concept.

While doing his Ph.D. research with Dan Gilbert at Harvard, **MATT KILLINGSWORTH INVENTED AN iPHONE APP CALLED "TRACK YOUR HAPPINESS."** Basically, the app would "ping" you at random times and ask questions about how you were feeling right now and what you were doing. The intent behind the app was to gather real time data on how people felt during their day and what they were doing to elicit those feelings.

What Killingsworth found was amazing. One of the questions he asked via his app was whether people were focused on what they were doing or if they were thinking about other things. This "mind-wandering" data point showed that for the over 15,000 people in more than 80 countries (with over 650,000 real-time reports), 47% of the time, regardless of what they were doing, people were thinking about things other than what they were doing right at the moment. Translated, it means that instead of thinking about the now, their minds were focused on other things.

While it might be only moderately surprising that most of us spend more than half our time occupying our minds with things other than what is happening in the now, Killingsworth's data showed something even more startling. He found that when people's minds wander, **THEY ARE SIGNIFICANTLY LESS HAPPY THAN WHEN THEY ARE FOCUSED ON THE PRESENT MOMENT**, regardless of what they were doing. Even something like sitting in traffic – which was rated one of the activities that made people least happy – people who were focused on the here and now reported being happier than people whose minds were wandering/daydreaming.

Killingsworth's study did not go so far as to state why people were happier when they were focusing on the present moment versus letting their minds wander, other than to suggest that most of us tend to think negative thoughts. **HOWEVER, HIS RESEARCH PROVIDES SOME OF THE FIRST REAL DATA TO SUPPORT WHAT PHILOSOPHERS, THEOLOGIANS AND SPIRITUALISTS HAVE BEEN SAYING FOR CENTURIES... FOCUSING ON THE PRESENT MOMENT IS ONE OF THE TRUE PATHS TO HAPPINESS.**

HEALING WITH LAUGHTER

An ancient proverb says: "**A MERRY HEART DOETH GOOD LIKE MEDICINE, BUT A DOWNCAST SPIRIT DRIES UP THE BONES.**" Hippocrates, the father of medicine, encouraged physicians to be of good cheer: "Use wit in your dealings with patients because dourness is repulsive both to the healthy and the sick."

Nothing makes most of us happier than when we laugh. A good laugh is a wonderful thing. It refreshes, relieves stress, generates positive emotions, promotes communication, strengthens group identity and cohesion, and benefits both the giver and receiver. In addition to these significant benefits, there is also evidence that laughter and humor promote good health.

There is an actual field of study in medicine about humor in medicine. It is called, "Gelotology" from the Greek root "gelos" meaning laughter.

WE CHANGE PHYSIOLOGICALLY WHEN WE LAUGH. When we laugh, we stretch muscles throughout our face and body, our pulse and blood pressure go up, and we breathe faster, sending more oxygen to our tissues. Laughing is a like a mild workout, and can even offer the same advantages as a workout.

But, once we stop laughing, the overall effect of the experience actually is relaxing. **ONE EARLY STUDY REPORTED THIS POST-LAUGHTER RELAXATION PERIOD CAN LAST UP TO 45 MINUTES. HEART RATE, RESPIRATORY RATE AND BLOOD PRESSURE ALSO DECREASE IN THE RELAXATION PERIOD.** This process of firing up one's engines in a pleasurable way, then immediately cooling down, can have a short-term stress-relieving and mind-clearing effect.

Studies are starting to isolate the effects of laughter or specific systems in the body in order to harness their effects.

INCREASED BLOOD FLOW: Researchers at the University of Maryland studied the effects on blood vessels when people were shown either comedies or dramas. After the screening, the blood vessels of the group who watched the comedy behaved normally – expanding and contracting easily. But, the blood vessels in people who watched the drama tended to tense up, restricting blood flow.

ENHANCED IMMUNE RESPONSE: Increased stress is associated with decreased immune system response. Some studies have shown that the ability to use humor may raise the level of infection-fighting antibodies in the body and boost the levels of immune cells, as well.

BALANCED BLOOD SUGAR LEVELS: A study of 19 people with diabetes looked at the effects of laughter on blood sugar levels. After eating, the group attended a tedious lecture (thankfully conducted by a professor other than myself). The next day the group ate the same meal and then watched a comedy. After the comedy, the group had lower blood sugar levels than they did after the lecture.

Better Relaxation and Sleep: The focus on the benefits of laughter really began with Norman Cousins' memoir, **Anatomy of an Illness**. Cousins, who was diagnosed with ankylosing spondylitis, a painful spine condition, found that a diet of comedies, like Marx Brothers films and episodes of Candid Camera, helped him feel better. **COUSINS SAID THAT TEN MINUTES OF LAUGHTER ALLOWED HIM TWO HOURS OF PAIN-FREE SLEEP.** Cousins subsequently established a Mind-Body Center at UCLA to study the effects of humor and the mind-body interactions on health and healing.

He who laughs, lasts.

— Mary Pettibone Poole

But, is Cousins' experience supported by science? Is it really true that something as basic and free as a good laugh can promote healing? Although the research on humor is still somewhat limited, there is evidence that individuals with chronic or terminal illnesses commonly use humor to promote healing, and that humor does have health benefits, such as improved pain tolerance and improved immune response.

At the 2005 meeting of the American College of Cardiology, Michael Miller, M.D., of the University of Maryland reported that in a study of 20 healthy people, provoking laughter did as much good for their arteries as aerobic activity. While Miller does not recommend that we forgo exercise in favor of laughing, he does advise that people try to laugh on a regular basis. The endothelium (the thin layer of cells that lines the interior surface of blood vessels and lymphatic vessels), he explains, regulates blood flow and adjusts the propensity of blood to coagulate and clot. In addition, it secretes assorted chemicals in response to wounds, infection or irritation, and plays an important role in the development of cardiovascular disease.

"The endothelium is the first line in the development of atherosclerosis, or hardening of the arteries," said Dr. Miller. "So given the results of our study, it is conceivable that laughing may be important to maintain a healthy endothelium, and reduce the risk of cardiovascular disease."

A 2008 STUDY FOUND THAT PARTICIPANTS WHO ANTICIPATED LAUGHTER EXHIBITED A REDUCTION OF CORTISOL, EPINEPHRINE (ALSO KNOWN AS ADRENALINE) AND A METABOLITE OF DOPAMINE, THREE TYPES OF STRESS HORMONES. Another research team found that those with heart disease were 40% less likely to laugh compared to comparable well people, suggesting the ability to laugh may have heart health implications. Humor as a form of complementary or alternative therapy also has been shown to have an overall emotionally positive influence on patients, helping to reduce anxiety and improve attitude.

> ***"Be careful about reading health books. You may die of a misprint."***
>
> *— Mark Twain*

Another small study of cancer patients in the rural Midwest found that over 87% were using at least one complementary intervention to cope with the stress of cancer. **THE SECOND MOST POPULAR INTERVENTION WAS THE USE OF HUMOR.** When it came to coping with their cancer and cancer treatment, participants identified humor as playing a major role in helping them through their illness.

Laughter, humor and happiness are a powerful combination when it comes to living healthier, longer lives. They also make our lives worth living. But, going back to the cancer patient study, there was one thing that came out in front of humor in terms of helping patients cope with their cancer and cancer treatment. **IT WAS PRAYER AND THE POWER OF FAITH IN HEALING**, which is the topic of our next RX+ Script.

SCRIPT 5

Practice your faith every day. Allow your belief in God to fill you with the joy of life.

THE BELIEF:

I AM LIVING EACH DAY IN THE FULLEST AWARENESS OF GOD IN MY LIFE.

Whether it is a personal belief in God and seeking God's will for your life — or simply being in awe of the wonder that is the universe – we are all part of something extraordinary. More and more medical research from leading hospitals and universities has shown conclusively that a belief in God really is good for you, and can make you healthier, happier... and help you live longer

A META-ANALYSIS OF 42 STUDIES EXAMINING 125,826 PEOPLE, PUBLISHED BY THE AMERICAN PSYCHOLOGICAL ASSOCIATION IN 2000, FOUND THAT ATTENDANCE AT A PLACE OF WORSHIP, WHETHER IT BE A CHURCH, SYNAGOGUE, MOSQUE OR TEMPLE CAN ADD EIGHT YEARS TO THE AVERAGE LIFE SPAN AND SIGNIFICANTLY IMPROVE HEALTH. Specifically, one study showed that religious people were one-third less likely to die after open-heart surgery than nonbelievers.

While private personal faith was found to be important, worshiping in a public place provided the most striking correlation between faith and good health. Public worship provides social contact and a strong support network and an overall positive environment, which can significantly reduce stress levels.

Duke University studied 4,000 people for four years and found that those who attended church weekly had a **28% LOWER MORTALITY RATE** overall when compared to those who didn't belong to a church community. The researchers also considered income, education, chronic diseases, other illnesses, health habits, exercise, smoking, drinking, body fat, social participation and psychological status. None of these factors explained the results. Church attendance was still an independent predictor and the strongest predictor of longevity.

Various theories have been put forth to explain this spiritual dimension to longevity. Physical explanations include people who are involved in religious groups benefit from the social networks they form. If they get sick, others look out for them. Religious beliefs may also lead to less risky behavior. In addition, a well-developed sense of spirituality may help people better cope with life's tough psychological demands.

In a later study of 1,700 older Americans, researchers at Duke University Medical Center found that those who attend religious services had stronger immune responses. About 60% of the men and women surveyed attended religious services at least once a week. Blood tests showed that regular attendees were less likely to have a high level of an immune system protein involved in age-related diseases.

> ***For God has not given us a spirit of fear***
> ***but of love power and a sound mind.***
>
> 2 Timothy 1:7

Psychoneuroimmunology

The relatively new science of Psychoneuroimmunology looks at the relationship between our thoughts and emotions and our bodies. Scientists have demonstrated that when we have a thought or feeling our brain produces neuropeptides, substances that allow brain cells to communicate with each other. Other cells in the body – most significantly the immune system – have receptors for these neuropeptides, and respond accordingly.

As Deepak Chopra, medical doctor and international speaker on the mind/body connection, says, "**Your immune system is continually eavesdropping on your internal dialogue.**" In his audio program, ***Magical Mind, Magical Body***, Chopra describes how different emotional states produce different chemical changes in the body. For example, tranquility produces the natural equivalent of Valium in our systems; nervousness produces adrenalin; and excitement produces interleukins, which, when manufactured chemically are hugely expensive anti-cancer drugs. He suggests a ride on Magic Mountain at Disneyland (so long as you like that kind of thing!) as an enjoyable and cheap way of producing these powerful chemicals - naturally!!

Research by Dr. H. Steven Greer, lecturer in Psychological Medicine at King's College Hospital Medical School, shows that those who react to a cancer diagnosis with hopelessness and helplessness have a much lower chance of survival than similar patients with who are more positive and possess a "fighting spirit." Dr. Greer is one of the founders of psycho-oncology as a sub-specialty in Britain, and along with Dr. Stirling Moorey, has developed a form of psychotherapy (called "adjuvant psychological therapy) that uses both cognitive and behavioral techniques to relieve depression and anxiety to help patients develop a fighting spirit towards their illness. Several randomized controlled studies have shown that adjuvant psychological therapy has improved the life of cancer patients significantly.

THE POWER OF PRAYER

For the devout, there never has been any question – prayer has the power to heal. Those who may not have been devout before are often inspired during a medical crisis to explore their faith and the power of prayer in much greater depth than ever before.

PRAYER CAN HAVE AN AMAZING IMPACT ON HEALTH. IT LOWERS BREATHING AND HEART RATE, AND CAN REDUCE BLOOD PRESSURE, ACCORDING TO STUDIES FOR THE NATIONAL INSTITUTES OF HEALTH. It also lowers levels of age-inducing stress hormones such as cortisol. Yet prayer also seems to have more extraordinary powers than this. Dr. William Kelley, who works in the field of nutritional and metabolic therapy, urges his patients to trust in God, to read the bible and to pray. He believes a positive attitude can play an enormous part in helping to diminish disease, and prayer is key to building and maintaining a positive attitude.

PRAYER FOR SELF HEALING

Numerous studies show that those who pray contemplatively or meditate – in both Western and Eastern traditions – can positively influence their health. There are many possible explanations for this, depending on your beliefs. First, those with strong religious beliefs of various traditions believe that by asking for healing through prayer, a loving and omniscient deity will respond. For many this is an unquestionable belief – important and hugely valuable to those who hold it – but difficult to understand and/or access for those who don´t.

> ***"Prayer is not an old woman´s idle amusement. Properly understood and applied, it is the most potent instrument of action"***
>
> - Mahatma Gandhi

Even for non-believers, there are points of view that do not require faith to explain the effectiveness of prayer. The act of prayer itself allows an individual to become quiet, release tension and let go of stress, which in and of itself has a positive physiological effect.

Dr. James Le Fanu, medical correspondent in the *Daily Telegraph*, describes an extraordinary piece of research by Professor Luciano Bernardi of the University of Padua. "There is a marked similarity in the physiological effects of chanted yoga mantras and the repetitive Latin of the Rosary Prayer, Ave Maria.... Surprisingly, they have a common thread, with the Rosary´s strong repetitive element having been introduced to Europe by the Crusaders who took it from the Arabs, who had in turn borrowed it from the Tibetan monks and yoga masters of India."

Professor Bernardi found that the reciting of the Rosary and yoga mantras slows the respiratory rate to six breaths a minute, which coincides with the rhythmic oscillation of nervous impulses controlling the heart rate. This synchronicity of respiratory and heart rate boosts oxygen in the blood, while improving circulation to the brain.

The increasing interest within the medical community to explore the science behind mystical traditions has yielded such significant results that more than 80 medical schools now offer courses on the role of religious practice and prayer in health.

Being Prayed For By Others

One of the most well-known studies about prayer by others was conducted by cardiologist Randolph Byrd and published in 1988. Byrd´s work took place with coronary care unit patients and was scientifically rigorous using a randomized, double-blind protocol. Over ten months, 393 patients in the unit were – with consent – admitted to a prayer group (192 patients) or a control group (201 patients). They were prayed for by Christians outside the hospital.

Neither the doctors nor the patients knew who was receiving prayer. When the study began the patients were all in a similar state of health. Over time the patients receiving prayer showed much better recovery rates than the others. The prayed-for patients were five times less likely than control patients to require antibiotics and three times less likely to develop pulmonary edema. While twelve of the control patients needed intubation to help with breathing, none of the prayed-for patients did.

Another impressive and more recent study was conducted in 1998 by Dr. Elisabeth Targ at the California Pacific Medical Center in San Francisco. Her study (again a double-blind experiment) was conducted with patients with advanced AIDS. Those patients receiving prayer had six times fewer hospitalizations, which were also of a significantly shorter duration than those people who received no prayer. Even Dr. Targ herself was surprised, "I was sort of shocked," she said in an interview with ABC News, "In a way it is like witnessing a miracle. There is no way to understand this from my experience and from my basic understanding of science."

Yet another study was conducted by Dr. Mitchell Krucoff at Duke University Medical Centre in North Carolina. He studied the effects of prayer on patients undergoing cardiac procedures such as catheterization and angioplasty. His findings show that patients receiving prayer had up to 100% fewer side effects from these procedures than people not prayed for.

In a study of 393 cardiac patients at San Francisco General Hospital, it was found that those who were prayed for by others needed fewer drugs and antibiotics and spent less time on ventilators. This was a scientifically conducted double-blind study in which none of the patients or nurses knew which patients were being prayed for.

A leading researcher and writer in this field is Dr. Larry Dossey, who has written extensively about the power of prayer. On his website, he cites examples from the plant and animal world. **WHEN BACTERIA ARE PRAYED FOR THEY GROW FASTER; WHEN SEEDS ARE PRAYED FOR, THEY GERMINATE QUICKER; WHEN WOUNDED MICE ARE PRAYED FOR THEY HEAL FASTER.** Dr. Dossey states, "I like these studies because they can be done with great precision, and they eliminate all effects of suggestion and positive thinking, since we can be sure that the effects are not due to the placebo effect."

Regardless of your spiritual beliefs, all of these studies show that faith – and practicing faith through prayer – can help you live a longer and healthier life.

℞+ SCRIPT 6

An Attitude of Gratitude

Practice an "attitude of gratitude" every day to consciously feed positivity in your life.

THE BELIEF:

I AM TRULY THANKFUL FOR EVERYTHING AND EVERYONE IN MY LIFE.

One of the best ways to cultivate and maintain a positive attitude is through an active practice of gratitude. Research has shown that being thankful confers a whole host of health benefits, from improved immune system, reduced heart rate, better sleep and enhanced mental stability.

"Thousands of years of literature talk about the benefits of cultivating gratefulness as a virtue," says University of California Davis psychology professor Robert Emmons. According to Emmons' research, grateful people – those who perceive gratitude as a permanent trait rather than a temporary state of mind – have an edge on the not-so-grateful when it comes to health. In an interview with WebMD, Emmons explains. **"GRATEFUL PEOPLE TAKE BETTER CARE OF THEMSELVES AND ENGAGE IN MORE PROTECTIVE HEALTH BEHAVIORS LIKE REGULAR EXERCISE, A HEALTHY DIET, AND REGULAR PHYSICAL EXAMINATIONS."**

Throughout history, philosophers and religious leaders have extolled gratitude as a virtue integral to health and well-being. Now, through a recent movement called positive psychology, mental health professionals are taking a close look at how virtues such as gratitude can benefit our health. And they're reaping some promising results.

Behavior: When it comes to practicing gratitude, the benefits can start at a young age. According to a 2012 study presented at the annual meeting of the American Psychological Association found that teens who are grateful (defined as having a positive outlook on life) are more well-behaved at school and more hopeful than their less-grateful peers. "More gratitude may be precisely what our society needs to raise a generation that is ready to make a difference in the world," study researcher Giacomo

Bono, Ph.D., a psychology professor at California State University, said in a statement about the research.

Strengthened Immune System: Grateful people tend to be more optimistic, which boosts the immune system. "There are some very interesting studies linking optimism to better immune function," says Lisa Aspinwall, Ph.D., a psychology professor at the University of Utah. In one study, researchers compared the immune systems of healthy, first-year law students under stress and found that, by midterm, students characterized as optimistic maintained higher numbers of blood cells that protect the immune system, compared with their more pessimistic classmates. Optimism also has a positive health impact on people with compromised health. In separate studies, patients confronting AIDS, as well as those preparing to undergo surgery **HAD BETTER HEALTH OUTCOMES WHEN THEY MAINTAINED ATTITUDES OF OPTIMISM.**

Mental Stability, Stress Management and Emotional Resilience: It seems counter-intuitive that we can feel gratitude even in the face of tremendous loss or tragedy, but the fact is, studies are finding that adversity actually helps us remember to be grateful. In a recent web-based survey tracking the personal strengths of more than 3,000 American respondents, researchers noted an immediate surge in feelings of gratitude after September 11, 2001.

Why would such a tragic event provoke gratitude? Christopher Peterson, PhD, the University of Michigan psychologist who posted the survey, attributes this surge in gratitude among Americans to a sense of increased belonging and connection to not only their community, but to the nation as a whole. Gratitude in the aftermath of 9/11 helped buffer people against the negative effects of stress, making them less likely to suffer from post-traumatic stress disorder.

Is the Glass Half-Full?

We have all heard the adage that optimists see a glass as half full and pessimists see it as half empty. But what if I were to challenge you to think a bit differently about the proverbial glass? **WHAT IF THE REAL PROBLEM WAS THAT THERE IS SIMPLY TOO MUCH GLASS?**

Gratitude, God and Wellness

The following quote is taken from a book originally **PUBLISHED IN 1910**. Written by Wallace B. Wattles in his book, **The Science of Being Well**. It is a summary on how we can use an "attitude of "gratitude" to promote health and well-being.

> *It is not merely the possession of faith, but the personal application of faith which works healing. You must claim health in the beginning, and form a conception of health, and, as far as may be, of yourself as a perfectly healthy person. And then, by faith, you must claim that you* ***ARE REALIZING*** *this conception. Do not assert with faith that you are going to get well; assert with faith that you* ***ARE*** *well.*
>
> *Having faith in health, and applying it first to yourself, means having faith that you are healthy; and the first step in this is to claim that it is the truth.*
>
> *Mentally take an attitude of being well, and do not say or do anything which contradicts this attitude. Never speak a word that assumes a physical attitude which does not harmonize with the claim:*
>
> *"I am perfectly well." When you walk, go with a brisk step, and with your chest thrown out and your head held up; watch that at all times your physical actions and attitudes are those of a healthy person.* **WHEN YOU FIND THAT YOU HAVE RELAPSED INTO THE ATTITUDE OF WEAKNESS OR DISEASE, CHANGE INSTANTLY; STRAIGHTEN UP; AND THINK OF HEALTH AND POWER. REFUSE TO CONSIDER YOURSELF AS OTHER THAN A PERFECTLY HEALTHY PERSON.** *Whenever you think of yourself, or of your advancing condition, give thanks to God.... Health from God is continually being urged upon you; and when you think of this, lift up your mind reverently to HIM, and give thanks that you have been led to the Truth and into perfect health of mind and body. Be, all the time, in a grateful frame of mind, and let gratitude be evident in your speech.*
>
> *Gratitude will help you to own and control your own field of thought...* **GRATITUDE HAS A TWOFOLD EFFECT: IT STRENGTHENS YOUR OWN FAITH, AND IT BRINGS YOU INTO CLOSE AND HARMONIOUS RELATIONS WITH GOD.** *You believe that there is one God from which all life and all power come, you believe that you receive your own life from God,* **AND YOU RELATE YOURSELF CLOSELY TO GOD BY FEELING CONTINUOUS GRATITUDE.**

Do not be anxious about anything, but in everything, by prayer and petition, with thanksgiving, present your requests to God.

Philippians 4:6

If we could take a laser and cut the glass down just above the level of the water, then both optimists and pessimists would have to agree the glass is completely full. The same could be said about switching from a negative to a positive mindset. **It is about shifting our perspective so we see how full our lives already are.**

It is true that many of us in the U.S. are struggling under our current economy. We are facing difficult times. But, before you complain about the price of gas or milk or anything else (thereby continuing the trend of negativity that pervades so much of our society), stop and re-think your situation. Even given the challenges we face, we are blessed. We live in one of the most affluent countries in the world. Consider how much of the rest of the world lives.

- **Almost half the world — over three billion people — live on less than $2.50 a day (that is $912.50 a year)**
- **At least 80% of humanity lives on less than $10.00 a day ($3,650 a year).**

From this perspective, we can truly be grateful that we can afford to feed ourselves and our families. Perhaps our dollar doesn't stretch as far as it once did. We might have to cut back on some of our indulgences — cook meals at home rather than dine out, rent movies instead of going to the theater, throttle back on our Starbucks habit, etc. But, given that one "FOURbucks" beverage is more than most people have to live on in a day, we should remember to savor the indulgences we do have even more. We have so much to be grateful for, if only we choose to accept it as is.

If we do not feel grateful for what we already have, what makes us think we would be happy with more?

Keeping a Gratitude Journal

One popular way to actively practice gratitude is by keeping a gratitude journal. The basic practice is relatively straightforward; take a little time a few times a week to record five or so things that you have experienced recently that you are grateful for. Keep your entries brief – just a sentence or two is sufficient. You can keep things simple ("I am grateful for waking up to another day") or more specific ("I am grateful that my child is no longer ill," or "I'm grateful for the food I have for dinner").

> ***Let the peace of Christ rule in your hearts, since as members of one body you were called to peace. And be thankful.***
>
> Colossians 3:15

To help you to get the maximum benefit from your gratitude journal, below are some tips taken again from the work of Dr. Robert Emmons, arguably the world's leading expert on the science of gratitude.

- ***Don't Just Go Through The Motions:*** Research by psychologist Sonja Lyubomirsky and others suggests that journaling is more effective if you first make the conscious decision to become happier and more grateful. If you are going to take the time to keep a gratitude journal, be grateful that you do.
- ***Get Personal:*** Focusing on **PEOPLE** to whom you are grateful has more of an impact than focusing on **THINGS** for which you are grateful.
- ***Try Subtraction, Not Just Addition:*** One effective way of stimulating gratitude is to reflect on what your life would be like without certain blessings, rather than just tallying up all those good things.
- ***Savor Surprises:*** Try to record events that were unexpected or surprising, as these tend to elicit stronger levels of gratitude.
- ***Don't Overdo It:*** Writing occasionally (once or twice per week) is more beneficial than daily journaling. In fact, one study by Lyubomirsky and her colleagues found that people who wrote in their gratitude journals once a week for six weeks reported boosts in happiness afterward; people who wrote three times per week didn't. "We adapt to positive events quickly, especially if we constantly focus on them," says Lyubomirsky. "It seems counterintuitive, but it is how the mind works."

Though he does have suggestions for how to keep a gratitude journal, Emmons also stresses that "there is no one right way to do it." There's no evidence that journaling at the start of the day is any more effective than journaling before you go to bed, for instance. And aesthetics really don't matter. "You don't need to buy a fancy personal journal to record your entries in, or worry about spelling or grammar," says Emmons. "The important thing is to establish the habit of paying attention to gratitude-inspiring events." If you are not the journaling type, you don't even have to write it down. You can begin and end each day by reflecting in your mind what you are grateful for in your life. The most important thing to remember is that practicing active gratitude can help reset your mind toward the good in life – making your days on this Earth more enjoyable and healthier.

Playing Guitar with Your Amigos

An American investment banker was taking a much-needed vacation in a small coastal Mexican village when a small boat with just one fisherman docked. The boat had several large, fresh fish in it. The investment banker was impressed by the quality of the fish and asked the Mexican how long it took to catch them. The Mexican replied, "Only a little while."

The banker then asked why he didn't stay out longer and catch more fish? The Mexican fisherman replied he had enough to support his family's immediate needs. The American then asked "But, what do you do with the rest of your time?"

The Mexican fisherman replied, "I sleep late, fish a little, play with my children, take siesta with my wife, stroll into the village each evening where I sip wine and play guitar with my amigos: I have a full and busy life, Senor."

The investment banker scoffed, "I am an Ivy League MBA, and I could help you. You could spend more time fishing and with the proceeds buy a bigger boat, and with the proceeds from the bigger boat you could buy several boats until eventually you would have a whole fleet of fishing boats. Instead of selling your catch to the middleman you could sell directly to the processor, eventually opening your own cannery. You could control the product, processing and distribution." Then he added, "Of course, you would need to leave this small coastal fishing village and move to Mexico City where you would run your growing enterprise."

The Mexican fisherman asked, "But Senor, how long will this all take?" To which the American replied, "15-20 years."

"But what then?" asked the Mexican. The American laughed and said, "That's the best part. When the time is right you would announce an IPO and sell your company stock to the public and become very rich. You could make millions."

"Millions, Senor? Then what?"

To which the investment banker replied, "Then you would retire. You could move to a small coastal fishing village where you would sleep late, fish a little, play with your kids, take siesta with your wife, stroll to the village in the evenings where you could sip wine and play your guitar with your amigos."

– Author Unknown

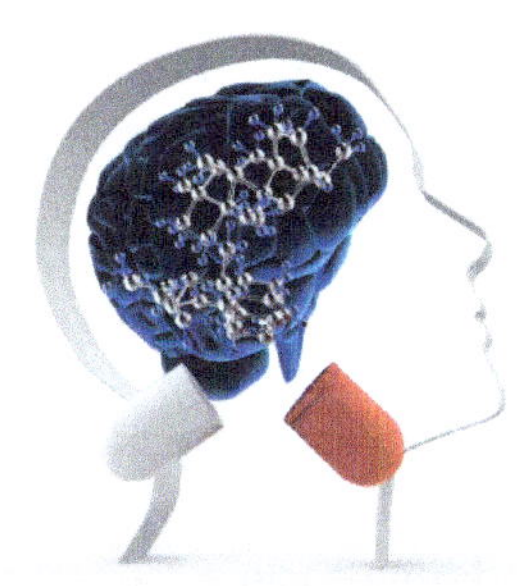

CHAPTER EIGHT

PUTTING IT ALL TOGETHER

As we come to the end of this book, it is time for a quick review of what we have learned and the important points we should take with us.

Let's begin with Part ONE: **THE CURRENT STATE OF HEALTHCARE.** In CHAPTER ONE: WHAT DO YOU REALLY WANT FROM HEALTHCARE? we learned that the most important thing any of us should want from our healthcare system is **NOT TO NEED IT!**

In CHAPTER TWO: THE UNBALANCED COST/BENEFIT RATIO, we revealed that for all the money we spend on healthcare in the country, we are not receiving any better care than people in other developed countries. In fact, the care we receive is far worse. The U.S. spends almost double the amount on healthcare (**$8,362 PER PERSON**) than Canada ($4,404 per person), France ($4,021 per person) and Germany ($4,332 person). For twice the price, you would think that we would live many more years than our European peers. However, in fact, our life expectancy is **TWO OR THREE YEARS LESS** than citizens of these countries.

The health cost per citizen in this country is estimated to continue to rise... and rise dramatically. By 2020, it is expected that the healthcare cost per person will be close to $14,000. **By 2050, that amount will have risen to an astonishing $80,000 per person!** The nature of healthcare must change. Our healthcare system must be reexamined not only from a cost perspective, but the very tenets of wellness must be challenged and revolutionized.

In Part TWO: **The power of Positive Belief** we highlighted an aspect of healthcare that is often sidelined or ignored. This critical aspect of wellness is often "talked at," but rarely leveraged to its fullest potential. Medical professionals have known about it for centuries. Theologians, philosophers and spiritualists have known about it for far longer than that. **The most ancient of healing practices is still one of the most important: the power of positive belief.**

In Chapter Three: The Power of Belief and the Placebo Effect, we argue that the placebo effect, which has been around as long as there has been medical practice, is proof positive that the mind truly has the power to heal and prolong our lives. The fact that time and time again a "sugar" pill has been able cure people of their ills, often better than an actual drug or other medical intervention, has so baffled the medical community that they have simply come to discard it as an aberration. They cannot explain it so they just do not acknowledge it beyond an annoying phenomenon they have to factor into their scientific research. It is this shallow and narrow-minded thinking that leads to the prescription of unnecessary drugs and surgical procedures.

But, the fact is, the placebo effect is real.

Time and time again, people cure themselves with no other help than a dummy pill or procedure to boost their brain into believing that they "should" get better. From the infamous Krebiozen and Ipecac examples of the past to antidepressants and even some surgical interventions today, the placebo effect plays a role in almost all medical treatment. The medical community's unwillingness or inability to openly harness the power of the placebo is endemic of what is wrong with the healthcare industry today. Most healthcare practices are intent on keeping the money and resources flowing into this multi-billion dollar industry rather than actively harnessing peoples' innate and powerful ability to heal themselves.

Part THREE: **The Power of a Positive Approach to Life** is dedicated to understanding the how the power of the mind has a huge impact over our health and longevity.

In Chapter Four: Positivity and Longevity, we outline a multitude of studies that link a positive mindset to living a healthful, long life. **They found that people with a positive mindset live between 8 to 15 years longer than people with a negative mindset.** More than any other factor, a positive approach to life influences your overall health and longevity.

In Chapter Five: Are You Positive? we challenge your degree of positivity by explaining how, since the dawn of man, our brains are essentially negativity engines. In order to keep us safe, we are internally wired to be on the lookout for things that might put us into harm's way.

The media relies on this negativity bias, capturing our attention with every headline that threatens our safety and well-being. But, all hope is not lost. **We have the ability to rewire our brains towards the positive.** No matter what our age, we can rewire our neural pathways through our actions and thoughts. We can program our "negative" mindsets into positive ones. The question is how?

In Chapter Six: How the Brain Works, we examine the science behind how our brain is constantly programmed, mostly at the subconscious level. **However, the more we become aware of the limiting beliefs we hold and how they affect our perception of the world, we can take more conscious control over how we perceive and act.**

Given the brain's ability to misinterpret information, add in information, edit out information and arrange information to meet our expectations, we must be on guard against Cognitive Consistency Syndrome, the tendency to readily accept information that confirms/conforms to our current beliefs, while ignoring or distorting information that does not conform. Perception can become even more altered when you add emotions to the mix, especially when it comes to a threat to our health. However, the more you understand about how your brain works, the more you can take control over your choices about your health and well-being.

Finally, in Part FOUR: **Your Prescription Positive** we presented six prescriptions (Rx+ Scripts) to help you raise and keep a positive mindset no matter what challenges or joys come into your life.

SCRIPTS

1. Self-Accountability

Be accountable for your life, especially your health choices. Take positive steps every day to secure a healthy and fully active life.

THE BELIEF:

I AM ACTIVELY TAKING CARE OF MY MIND, BODY AND SPIRIT.

2. Manage Your Stress

Consciously and actively manage the stress in your life. Do what you can to reduce stressors and leverage the stress you have to your advantage.

THE BELIEF:

I AM MORE THAN CAPABLE OF HANDLING ALL ASPECTS OF MY LIFE EASILY AND POSITIVELY.

3. Focus on Positive Relationships

Build and maintain positive relationships in your life with others, and especially yourself.

THE BELIEF:

I PLACE A PRIORITY ON MY RELATIONSHIP WITH MYSELF. I HAVE STRONG POSITIVE RELATIONSHIPS WITH OTHERS.

4. Cultivate Happiness

Actively seek happiness in your life. Recognize that happiness is a choice dependent not on circumstances, but on belief.

THE BELIEF:

I CHOOSE TO BE HAPPY TODAY AND EVERY DAY.

5. Have Faith

Practice your faith every day. Allow your belief in God to fill you with the joy of life.

THE BELIEF:

I AM LIVING EACH DAY IN THE FULLEST AWARENESS OF GOD IN MY LIFE.

6. An Attitude of Gratitude

Practice an "attitude of gratitude" every day to consciously feed positivity in your life.

THE BELIEF:

I AM TRULY THANKFUL FOR EVERYTHING AND EVERYONE IN MY LIFE.

The Final Word

To summarize this book in one sentence:

Your beliefs to a very large degree determine your health, wellness, longevity and quality of life.

That's it! It is not your genes or even your environment that determines your health. **It is how you think!** If you have a strong positive mindset and believe that you will live a long and healthy life, than that is what you will do. If you are ill or injured, the more you can fix your thoughts to the positive, the more you will be able to heal. If you doubt this for a second, go back to Chapter Three and reread the stories and studies about the placebo effect (i.e., the "Belief Effect").

You have opportunities to use and leverage the "Belief Effect" every day. Think about the vitamins and nutritional supplements you take. Do they contribute to your health? Possibly... especially if you **think** they are making you healthier. What about the baby aspirin your doctor asks you to take every day. Does it have a therapeutic effect? Probably. It "works" even better if you **believe** it is helping to keep you healthy. Even that simple 30 minute daily walk that your doctor has suggested contributes to your overall health can be magnified if you use your mind's eye to "visualize" how your walk is having a positive impact on your heart, lungs and your overall health and well-being.

Consider the following sequence of statements regarding your thoughts:

- Today, you are a product of the thoughts you had yesterday.
- Who you are tomorrow is a product of your thoughts today.
- If you want to change your life, you must change your thoughts.
- When you change your thoughts, you change your beliefs.
- When you change your beliefs, you can dramatically change your life.
- Be very intentional when it comes to your thoughts and beliefs.

I foresee a time in the future when health conscious individuals and the best physicians together **WILL EMBRACE THE POWER OF THE MIND AS THE PRIMARY WAY TO STAY HEALTHY...** and the primary path to restoring health.

PRESCRIPTION POSITIVE AND ALL THAT IT ENTAILS IS A STEP IN THAT DIRECTION. This book was created to empower people – you – to embrace the awesome opportunity and responsibility you have over your health and longevity by leveraging the power of your mind. Decide how to take your daily dose(s) of the six RX+ Scripts, and you will be well on your way to leveraging your beliefs for a longer and healthier life.

About The Author

Richard C. Huseman, Ph.D. has been an academic for most of his life, having served as professor, department head and dean at various universities including long-term assignments at the University of Georgia and the University of Central Florida, plus a two-year sabbatical at the University of Southern California and a major leadership development project with the University of California at Berkley.

He now is the founder and CEO of an executive coaching firm dedicated to providing leadership development and performance coaching to leaders at every level. Dick is a highly recruited keynote speaker, and consultant. Working with companies like AT&T, Coca-Cola, ExxonMobil, Deloitte, IBM, as well as several healthcare systems across the country, his focus has been in the areas of knowledge management, Relational Intelligence®, change leadership, and leadership development.

Dick has authored 21 books, including his most recent works, **Relational Intelligence®: The New Smart** (2012), and **How the Brain Works: Unlock the Secret to Great Leadership** (2009). He is the author/coauthor of more than 100 articles and professional papers.

Dick has been a student of health and longevity for most of his life, dedicating a great deal of time and study to the study of health and wellness. This book stems from his own personal pursuit for a happy, long life and the ability to pass what he has learned to his family, especially his seven grandchildren.

For more information about:

and related presentations, workshops, seminars, training programs, assessment instruments, and quantity discounts for this book, please visit:

www.PrescriptionPositiveRX.com

READER'S NOTES:

CPSIA information can be obtained at www.ICGtesting.com
Printed in the USA
LVOW01s0924260813

349602LV00006B/10/P